CAN YOU KEEP A SECRET?

CAN YOU KEEP A SECRET?

To my mother, Maria, my father, Ricky, my brother Alan, and my dog Krane, thank you for making team Nelson a dream come true. This dedication is not much, but remember a story tells a thousand words. Have fun with ours.

P.S: Alan, rockstar, agent 2364, I love your writing. I'm passing this story to you. Stop being so stubborn and listen to mom and dad sometimes. You are always right, but they always know what you are up to. Whenever you feel like crying, smile. Whenever you get angered, laugh. God is watching your spirit and he knows your name. Talk to him, and don't forget to mention me. I love you handsome. Talk to you in a minute.

Welcome to Can You Keep A Secret...Don't be scared, turn the page.

CAN YOU KEEP A SECRET?

What if I told you…I am a dream. People always say dream big, well why not think big? I think that's what loss my self- control, or maybe was it that dirty deed to my missing piece that defined my unity.

I think of myself as to where God is. My thoughts start there. They elevate each time I kneel and pray. Sometimes I fret of going too far that I'll never return. Somedays I'm never the same. He shows me different perspectives throughout the years that I've been praying. Everyday is a new day for me. I never know where he'll take me. He's the fun part about me. I learn something new, meeting him each day. It really is a blessing to see the amazing works of me through the eyes of him. Although I cannot see God's vision, I catch a glimpse of the future here and there through my ears. He speaks, and I lay at attention. My best years are spent on my bed prying my thoughts apart. It is my only peace in such an confined world. The world is never too big for my dreams, but maybe this bed is. I find myself contemplating on it way too often. Maybe I should get off it more often and stop judging myself into suppressing my

CAN YOU KEEP A SECRET?

thoughts. Ever curl has to set right, and every pattern has to make an appearance. I cannot be without my features looking to par. I will not be without my essence. My figure is not apart of my dream, but it is a dream to watch it flow. No S curve or coke bottle preference, just enough weight to where I can hold myself up to stand. It's hard being a woman, the ratio for the mind to my emotions is inexplicably rare. I cannot walk outside wearing my beauty without a man touching my significance with his breath. Sometimes I just want to go for coffee, and other times to sit and read a nice book on a wonders day. It's like those times as a woman, people start to view you different. Men try to teach you different.

It was the start of that day where my first thought was work. It should have been God, but how busy can we get? My motive was to get there and get off. Of course, I would enjoy the little things while I am there. Then again, how busy can we get. Work is work when it's not your soul's passion, or your career. I would rather be in the mirror rubbing through my locs. Is that too vein? Working through the hours in the day just makes you think about yourself and what you have going on. Customers come through and through and that's all they are. No

5

appeal to their title, no personal connection. Even if you were to make a connection, how personal can you get behind a barrier. I'm not asking for it to be broken down. I just want my emotions to be respected. People care but not deep enough, when conversing with one another. I am always watching the simplicity of missing vital details in a conversation. These days make me feel like it is just a simple, structured, organized way of talking. There's no depth to saying hello, or no critical thinking behind how are you. What if every day you meet someone, you start with a different sentence you never spoke with before. It might throw you off balanced, but now you can tap into a different train of thought, or maybe even a specific realm of being. Now your reaction becomes natural and not so stern. Now I can take your emotion serious because it's out of the ordinary. Your question for me made you think a little bit harder for my response. This is why work for me goes so smoothly. Not a day goes by that it isn't any different. I know what to expect. I get stressful tasks but I just do it with ease. I learn the ropes and connect the dots. Simple task for a complexed mind is no task for the unforgiven. Different we appeal to be, but all we want is love. A little love never hurt anybody. Life should be taken more slowly. Why not? I'll be able to breathe more, caress my words more, maybe even to also define my place in this sanction just a little bit more. Why can't we change the clocks around, instead of setting it to a different time when the seasons change. Maybe then time would not be so "stressful" or be the center of our attention.

Of course, I change my feelings throughout the day. It's a must. I can't be positioned into one system the entire day. Some days I have a hard time working, or a hard time focusing on my life because my thoughts for my sanity is too deep. I change a quick thought by making it into a rhythm I can listen to. Instantly, a different thought you questioned you could not control. Meeting someone different every day and realizing that for some, it is the same conversation just different words. For a one in a million, it takes a beat of time.

You make me think progression even when there is success. It was this one guy that caught my eye in college. I was studying pre-law, while he was a pre-med student. With my mind, he took me.

I am my last semester in before graduating with my AA. One of my class requirements was to take up a physical education class. It was an online class, so I had a bit of leeway. There was still obligations just like any other class, and I had to "check in" online at least every other day. Just like clockwork huh. I dreaded it. Not that I didn't enjoy working out, it was just the thought of having to go to the gym every single day for 50 minutes like clockwork. Plus, who said I didn't like the way I looked. I'm not a big fan of people telling me what to do. Why do I have to work out to fit the statistic of a fit body, when I can create my own word for it because I am a specific body? Whatever. The good thing about it was I didn't have to show up in physical form to take this course. I went to the gym on my own time. I went on different days and different times, just to make it look as if I am doing the proper workout for each day. Each day there would be numerous of us in there talking about the same thing and about the same class. One day I went in a signed the roster for my checking in date. Filling out as usual with calculating the same number of exercises. Then all of a sudden a disturbance.

"What's a pretty lady like you doing single", he says.

I continue to write up my workout for the day and say, "What makes you think I'm single?"

CAN YOU KEEP A SECRET?

There was no answer for at least 30 seconds, so I looked up. I see this voluptuous body, deep chocolate, and soft eyes of a man.

"Why is he looking at me", I think to myself.

I stare at him much longer to figure out why he must stare at me with those seeping eyes. Then I remembered he asked me a question.

"Oh, what was the question again?"

I don't know what came over me. At this age, guys don't really hold my interest anymore. They just become bland with their child like manner, but him..

He laughs, "I asked if I could have your name."

"Boy bye. No you didn't. You asked what was a lady like me doing single, am I correct."

"If you knew, then hahaha. Okay yes mam I did."

"Just so you know, I'm not interested", I said with a wink.

I mean he was cute. What was I supposed to do. I wasn't interested, I think. I go and proceed with my days workout. Going from machine to machine, I catch him glance over at me a couple of times. Why was this bothering me, much less making me anxious. My head was being tested, and he was surely clouding my mind. This is not healthy. I barely even said two words to him. Maybe I should have given him my name. Maybe then I won't feel as guilty for wanting him. Shoot! Did I say that out loud. Forgive me lord, but there is a beautifully, well-done, handsome man sitting at the front entrance, and I can't contain my hands to lift these weights. My I don't know what has come over me. Give me space lord and strength to finish this workout. I amp up the music in my headphones and let the feeling pass me by. Then again an upbeat song comes on, and I feel like moving my hips. I must leave this gym at once. Please tell me, it has been 50 minutes. My next machine is the treadmill. Oh my, and my ass is going to be jumping all around. I mean I do have some weight on me, so I don't know how this is going to look. Next time I'll wear sweats.

"Oh get yourself together, no one's worried about you and your Harlem shake", I say in my head. I continue. Only fifteen minutes on here, and then I am racing for the door. I start to run on an incline, and I'm loving this new feeling of working out. It's like extra wind has hit my chest, and I am able to breathe again. Pandora is playing the right songs without me getting emotional or insecure, so I guess I can enjoy this run. I feel uplifted and rejoiceful. I begin bobbing my head to the beat. Swaying my hips back and forth as I keep up with the music. Okay, I feel like myself again. This is great. Thank you God, you sure do work fast. My ten minutes is up. Now it's time for a cool down, so I walk for the rest of the five.

"Wow, what a great workout", I say to myself as I walk back to the front counter to fill out my "check out" form. Yep, he's still there, touching me with his eyes like before. He has to sign my sheet, verifying that I worked out as instructed. I hand it to him with a smile. He signs his name and returns it back to me.

"Oh so your name is Vincent", I say reading his signature.

I gather my things, place them in its respectable box and close the cabinet shut. As I turn to walk out, I remembered something. I look back over my shoulder and say "My name's Jah by the way. Hope to see you again Vin."

The next couple of weeks were just like so. Me coming in giving him the eyes, and him signaling me back. I was for sure going to ace my course, especially with Vincent's support. He gives me one beautiful look, and I'm amped for the rest of the session. One day was different though. I hit all my marks, checked in at an appropriate time and walked out like I usually do. It wasn't until I made a run to Wal-Mart that everything changed. I get a Facebook request from a guy named Vincent Gilbert. His name does not ring a bell, and I can't figure out who this might be. I click on the guy's profile picture and it's HIM. Oh my goodness, the guy from the gym. But how?

How does he know my full name? I never gave him that much. Oh wow, he must have looked real hard to find all of this out. This is real suspect. I am going to deny. Before I could press the button, a chat pops up with his name on it.

"Geese this is strange. What could he possibly want at this time of the night. I mean I know he was feeling me a little bit, but this is next level."

The chat says, "Hey you left your campus card at the gym. I'll keep it here for you for when you return."

"Whew, dodged that bullet. That would have been..never mind, let me just reply."

I call him through the messenger app.

I pick up the phone laughing, "Hey, oh wow. I completely thought the total opposite of you, so let me apologize"

CAN YOU KEEP A SECRET?

"Oh. Wait. You thought? No no no. I am for sure not that kind of person. I just saw your card here at the front desk as I was closing my station down. I'm glad it was you though."

"Of course you did ahaha. Well now you know who I am. Well, kind of."

"I'll see you back at the gym. Have a goodnight."

No he didn't. He really just ended the conversation without any flirtatious input. I gather my thoughts. This can't be true. That's it. No, can I have your number? Well, I know it's coming soon, so I will just wait. This could just be who he is though. Maybe he isn't like most and try to move too forward with a woman…hahaha yeah right that was funny. He's a guy.

I pray to myself, "God please keep an eye out for this young fellow, amen."

I meet my girls at the coffee shop the next day.

"Yes girl, and then he just hung up the phone"

"You sure you're not just over reacting J", Brooke said.

"Yeah maybe he didn't want to be that guy", replies Shay.

CAN YOU KEEP A SECRET?

"Alright, well yal sit here and play booboo the fool, while I go grab some coffee", I said as I walked over to the register.

"Make sure it's black", Brooke replies.

I look back with a silly grin on my face.

I order myself a grande hot medium roast coffee with almond milk, a dash of toffee nut flavoring, and three creams with two sugars. I pay, and proceed back to the table. As we're siting, the guy closest to me takes his shoes off and folds his leg on top of his lap. All what is in my preview is fungus, dead skin, and ash. What a disgrace. I shake my head in disgust.

"Can we move this conversation to outside yal?", I say as I slowly get up with maneuvering my body to not touch the guy's foot.

"For what reason J, it's windy out", Shay states.

I nod my head over to the left and have my eyes to follow. They catch my drift and got up fast.

"We need to plan another girls' trip", Shay said.

"Yeah right you guys are the last one's to be talking about a trip, since you all have lives of your own now. I can't wait to be like yal when I grow up, hahaha", I replied.

"When has that ever stopped us", Brooke said.

"Okay, so where to? I'm thinking Cali"

The conversation runs short, seems to that we all have to go to work soon.

"Love you"

"Love you"

"Love yal, bye"

Another day at a job where I am not fulfilling my passion, just scrubbing floors, nothing new. I won't be negative though and state that this job isn't for me because it pays the little bills that I do have, and it is putting me through college. I have a promising job after I graduate, so how much really could I hate about it? There's things that you must do throughout your time here on earth. I must make my job the best of what it is and have the grace of God to carry me through.

I get home from a long days day of thinking up of nothing more but to pursue my dream. A dream that I haven't thought of yet, but something that gives me life in a world with no ceilings. I write in my journal:

CAN YOU KEEP A SECRET?

I'm not sure yet what my dream in life means to me. I know, however, that I must make something shake in this world. I must complete a fantasy or an equilibrium of my ancestors' passion. What will it be though. I'm in school for numerous of things. I receive my degree in communications this summer, and then I will go forth with getting my BS in marketing. There must be more to life though than a sheet of paper, or is it that all that this world sums around. My passion is writing. I can vividly sit in a room and reminisce for hours and have no complaints. It's something I love doing journal. If I could drop out of school at this moment and become a writer, I would. I don't know. I guess the college life teaches you a good bit. Actually now that I think of it, it prepares you for precise knowledge to come. You never get your blessing straight forward. It always comes in a curve, but not as sneaky as a snake. Sometimes when I'm talking to my friends, journal, I think of what I have learned in class and use it to converse with them. I like to elevate those around me because what good am I, if can't put back in the universe what I consciously took from it. Also, like the good ole' saying journal, "You're as good as the company you keep." Therefore if we're not maximizing our strengths in conversations to come, than how am I to speak to someone eloquently about why I should be hired in their company. We can help each other. All we are to do is gravitate towards one another and let God speak for us. That's how the mind works. Gravity, per say, is always right side up. I just hope one day I wake up on the right side. Let the universe take me to sleep, goodnight journal.

Chapter 2

"I guess I didn't scare you away after all, welcome back."

"Don't you forget I am here just for class you know."

"I know, but one day I'll get your number. It pinches my spine to see you walk by everyday and not know who you are. There's something about you I must know."

"Well you get me to smile every time I come into the gym, so there's a start."

"So what are you to work on today, abs?"

"I think I'll do some cardio and upper body exercises."

"I do not my best this time not to stare."

I start on the treadmill this time since it got me amped up the last time. This is the best therapy. I may lose weight, gain weight, or maybe even stay the same, but I do know my mindset changes every time I step foot into this facility. It almost makes me feel important like I am destined to do something. Who would of thought that I would love this class this semester. The mind is a beautiful thing when you put it to work. Exercising not only my mind, but as well my ability to think a little bit clearer. To not have someone cloud your thoughts all the time is a sensation I must attach myself to. Could I even withstand a relationship right now? It's not my focus, but it does indeed cross my mind often. Then I think again, and I say yes. I am in tuned with myself, learning my potential and rave of talents. I am in love all over again, and this time it is with myself and my health. The music changes to a love song. I walk to its pace. There's symbolism in seeing things come true, seeing first hand your personal situations come to life. I believe the love word begins with your epistemology of yourself. Discovering pieces and paths without having to look in the mirror is the logic of self. I have short hair and no eyebrows, and I think what a nice roulette.

Time to switch to some weight lifting. Strength training pervades my path of advantageous secrets. One pull, one tug two lifts at a time. I'm sweating off my desires to aspire of nothing more than to be complete. A rush filled with patience. With patience, I take my load up. It doesn't matter how much I can lift, but the ultimate lift through my mind. I don't know what it is, but I have the epitome of taking care of my mind first. I know of loosing it once before, so I'm careful of how I

19

manipulate it. Even with certain songs, I am not able to function through because they're so fast pace. With those songs, they barely give you enough time to think about the next lyric. Not that a song must be filled with guesses, but I at least want my mind to relax on a song's harmony. There's a difference between an upbeat song that gives you energy, than a song that makes you think it's a remedy when really it has no symphony. I need a song to relieve me from my doubts when the weights become a barrier for my body. I sum up to why I don't listen to much of what is popular, but to what is historical and memorable. I switch to jazz for my cool down.

Walking back to the front counter, I feel ten pounds lighter. Maybe not so much to the aspect of loosing weight, but my mind is now a blank slate.

"How was your workout?", Vincent asked.

"Well you should know, you were staring at me the whole time remember."

"This might be too forward, and stop me if it is, but can I take you out for lunch sometime?"

Thinking to myself:

CAN YOU KEEP A SECRET?

He asked me out for lunch instead of dinner. What a nice game of toss he's playing. Everyone knows having dinner would lead to the bedroom. Maybe he thought the same, and wanted to go with the safer route. Is he really a difference in my life God, or am I just that gullible. I should probably give him a break. I mean he did try. After standing there with a blank stare on my face for almost too long, I decide to give him my answer,

"Yes, just say when."

I walked off not realizing what I said and realized that I needed to say more. I walk back.

"I guess I'm the one that needs to say "when", I said.

"So you're not that good at these type of things are you"

"Listen when you get out of a bad relationship, and start fresh with yourself, you start to love yourself again. You realized the only hope you have left is for yourself. I'm not stating that my family was not there to listen. However, you know how us millennials are. We like to deal with our issues on our own. I am at a place between commitment and comfort. By this I mean, I have shielded my mind from this type of thinking, until I was ready and fully recovered. I'm not recovered completely, but I am recovering. I have been through single, complicated, disturbed, disgust, and now it's back on me. My back is on me. Understand, I am the one doing the lifting. If and when I ever hand it over to you, I will lift you up too. I know I am giving you a lot of information right now. I want you to know I am too grown for this. If you are here for temporarily measures, a quick set up, or anything in between, please don't ever look my way again. Maybe it is that you are a guy, and you cannot wrap your head around what I am saying, so you will persist anyway. However, I am telling you once again, making it very clear in my soft but shaken voice, I don't want you. I'll give you this one date though. If you can make me laugh, you can surely make me cry, so please be careful with the way that you speak to me. I am a woman. This may work out, but only if you do not forget these words as I speak them to you today. I am fragile, yet wholesome. I am beauty, yet plastic. I have been broken, yet I can still beat your ass…with a bat.

"So, we can do lunch around let's say 1230 at my favorite wing spot, Friday before I go into work. I'll text you with the details. Chow my love.'"

CAN YOU KEEP A SECRET?

Thursday rolls around, and I decided to facetime my good friend Brooke, who is about to leave and go back to her home in California. I need her help picking out something quite sexy yet sophisticated for this date.

"I thought you didn't even like him", she says as I try on some clothes.

"I mean I don't know you know. Out of all the other guys I have curved, he seems to catch my eye. Maybe it's going to be different this time. Oh goodness, I can't believe I said that. 'This time' really? Is that just not a sign for me to not do this?"

"Girl c'mon, let me see what you have picked out."

I walk out with this collard brown blouse on and a flowery print skirt.

"No really, really, this is what you want to wear."

"No c'mon, what's with the way I am dressed."

"Jah, you look like a grandma."

"I think it's cute, and plus it is much more comfortable than a tight dress that will probably ride up this fat...ugh do you really not like it? I can unbutton the blouse a little bit to spice it up, no?"

"Try on the loose jumpsuit and tie a blazer around the front", she suggests.

" I guess it's not that bad for a lunch date. What if I wear a short sleeve blouse with the.."

"Nooo"

"Well my mind is made up and that is what I am going with. You've been so helpful for today. Who can I call today to rave about your customer service?"

"You're such a.."

"I know, but that is why you love me."

I get home. Mom has made her famous curry chicken, but I skip dinner and go straight into my room. Struggling to find a pen, I was itching to write something down:

Hey journal, I have come from a full day of shopping even though I only bought one outfit. I kind of curse Brooke out during the process, or she swore me down. I'm not real sure, but I had tons of fun. I think. Well, you know how I am journal don't give me that look. My nerves are starting to get to me again. This date, journal, what am I to do? I haven't been on one of these since you know like never. No one has ever taken me out on a real date. It has always been me paying, me coming up with an idea, and me laying down on my back to give into this nut of a job that doesn't even respect the fact that I am a woman with delicacy. Well, there was this one guy that took me on a real date. I forgot where we went. Oh wait, the attic. never mind journal I think I am just getting way ahead of myself. Do you really think this guy could be someone special? I told him if he ruins my fruit, I'd have to swing on him. I'm just over the b.s. I don't need a guy, and to be honest journal, I don't think I want one either. Hey, if I must be optimistic, I will say he smells nice. That's a start right. He doesn't have that stench of a rebel, or a stench of a hungry garden tool. It is more like an aroma of a fresh dandelion. Those don't even have a smell. You see where I am going with this journal. It's this guy. He makes me all fresh in the head again. My thoughts are clear of him, when I am away from him. It's like I can put him out of my mind like that. Whenever, I get close to his scent, I'm all girly again. Ew, when have I ever been girly right? I know. I guess I'll go to sleep now journal since you are blurring your lines. Goodnight babe. Pray for me.

Friday

I wake up super early to start my day. I have class at nine, so I get dress for both class and my lunch date. Wow, I haven't did this in a while. This dating thing is new to me. I just know I am supposed to look cute enough and appropriate. From the looks of my outfit, I have nothing to worry about, and my skirt isn't grandma long. I don't know what Brooke was talking about. I look fine wearing it. I stop day dreaming and get up to wash my face and brush my teeth. Next is my favorite part, makeup. This should take me no time, since I shaved off my eyebrows. I got tired of doing them every morning. What can I say? Going through my favorite products, and I'm thinking to keep it very soft and pretty, today. Everything is gliding on quite simply this morning. This might be a good day after all.

I get to class. This class always interest me because you never know what the professor is going to lecture. This is my Accounting Class. All we talk in this class is numbers, but you'd be surprise at how numbers can flip. I not only know how to save and spend money, but I as well know how to invest it.

CAN YOU KEEP A SECRET?

That's the beauty of making money. I can make it in my sleep and I have the knowledge to do so. Though, my interest is entrepreneurship. I really don't see myself working for anybody too long. It's not my thing. I love sleep, and I also love to wake up when I want to without needing to punch in and out of the clock. Kids and teenagers younger than me have figured it out with the little schooling they have. Why would I not be able to do great things, and I am at a college level. I take out my notes for this one. One semester from graduating with my AA. You really think I am not going to reach for the stars. It isn't a master's degree or a doctorate. However, it is something with my name on it that I can call my own. Organization is key to steps to accounting. Well, duh. Someone else's dirty money won't be left on my hands. My organization skills are well. Let's just skip to lunch.

My favorite wing spot besides the wing spot in the food court at the mall. Buffalo Wild Wings is my second home. I don't even have to wait 'til he gets there. I get out the car to see him all dappered down with flowers in his hands, dandelions to be exact. How, I wonder. I walk up to him and ask what his choice for dandelions was.

"I figured since you never done anything like this before that I'd be the first and hopefully the last. I chose dandelions because I want you to wish upon as many of them as you can. Maybe then, I could help you see all of them come true", he replies.

"How will you know what I have wished for though?"

"The universe will tell me", he saids.

"Oh so you're a believer! First impression is everything, and that is good to know."

We walk inside, and I tell him I prefer booths. Mannerisms are key, so I watch the way he talks to others and not just myself. Everything is looking good so far. He is super polite and kind with his words. We sit down. He asked if he could order for me. I thought it was a little strange because he is literally doing everything I have never seen before. It's not a bad feeling, it is just different. Of course, I tell him he can order for me. I tell him I would like ten mild wings, all flats, non-breaded with a glass of vodka and lemonade mixed. He was shocked by my order. I think the drink got him all excited.

"So you like to drink?", he says.

"I think it's more for the nerves", I laughed.

He said, "Oh no, with a combination like that, you must know your liquor."

"Guilty. What do you like to drink or do you not?"

"Oh no I do, but I like a little more of what is going to put some hair on your chest"

I flutter my eyes at his statement.

"Ahaha whatever. Then, so, what will you order?"

"To be honest I have never tried BWW's wings before."

"Shut up! This small town. I mean what else would you eat?", I said.

"Burgers is my meal of choice. For you, however, I will give this place a try", he said with wink.

I think to myself that he better not give me too much of those soft eyes. I can conduct myself, and no we are not having sex anytime soon. As for my heart though, it's slowly dancing around this cold barrier I had when I first me him. I don't know. The more I talk to him, the less worried I am about him trying me in a disrespectful way. We have drinks to calm our nerves, so we are sharing a lot of laughs. This is good. This is mellow.

"What are you thinking over there?", he says.

"Nothing really. I'm just enjoying my view."

"So, I did some research on this place and I hear that they have a burning hot wing contest that almost nearly everyone tries at least once. I figure this would be the perfect time to 'spice things up', make this date a little fun, and try it with you. Yes?"

"You're so corny, but somehow you make me laugh every time with your puns. Yes, I would definitely enjoy an adventure with you. I am scared though."

"Now I don't want to pressure you into anything. I am paying for everything. I just want you to have fun, so drink and eat as much as you want. Okay?"

"Wow, thank you for your generosity. I know this is cliché, but I feel like a missing piece has been filled, and I don't necessarily think I'm talking out of the way or too forward for that matter. However, all you guys are nice and buttery, when you first meet a young woman. Converse with me for a couple of months and let's see if he feels the same. I could be wrong though. I really want to vibe on this new feeling.

"It's just this feeling, however, that I haven't felt ever, and you seems to have captured whatever it is, perfectly. I think a lot of the times us ladies like to forgive our past, but never accept the forgetting part. Why is that? I mean yeah sure someone broke your heart and it feels bad, indeed it really does. It's like raucous in your mind and disturbances in your heart almost as if you can't breathe. I've been through the tribulations more than the trials, and I'm sure you feel the same. My question is, however why do we stop? Why do we leave the pieces on the floor waiting for someone else to pick them up? What if someone never picks them up, and they just walk by looking at us hopelessly. Then what? I believe it's our job sometimes to handle the situations with God before we step into another relationship. You can't simply move on to someone else as quickly as you left some person and think that those same problems won't occur."

"I can't get over how open minded you are, you really are an open book. Most young women won't even begin to process half of what you just thought of off rip.", he says.

"But hey, that's okay", I reply.

"No, of course it is. I wouldn't think no further of it. Let me put it in more light terms. We naturally think selfishly because we want so much for ourselves; which is okay. It is in our human nature to think self-first. Though, woman are the power behind the world. You guys can do amazement with just the tip of your fingers. Why not males value the right of a woman, or the concept of the woman starting with the heart. Sometimes, it makes me highly upset seeing young woman going through so much at a young age. I mean why? If you choose, as a guy, for a lady to be in your life than why not hold her to her pedestal. For Christ sakes, so what if it looks feminine, soft, or comes across as sensitive. Why can't we be sensitive to our woman, you guys are the nature of the universe. Woman bring life into this world effortlessly. It still amazes me to this day that you all are pregnant for nine months at some point in your life. The emotion that you all bring. It's magical to say the less. I admire your beauty mam. For you, I have to look from a distance because there is a such thing as getting lost in it. I don't want to get lost with you yet take my time with you. It has to make sense and come natural."

"I'll leave you on that last word, our wings are here", I reply.

I'm looking at these wings and they are dripping with hot sauce. Looking at them makes me want to run for the ocean and soak there. I don't know if I am up for this challenge. I actually would rather run up a hill, but I'll settle with what is in front of me. Instead of doing how many wings we can eat in a given time, we see who can eat the most wings. From there, we dive in.

"Oh my gosh this is intense", I shout.

"To be honest with you, I can't even get over the smell. It's so reviling", he replies

"One wing down, aahhh, okay I'm winning."

One wing after the other, and we're tearing through these vicious creatures. Sweat is dripping down our face and eyes. This is not a great feeling at all. I feel like I'm having diarrhea in my mouth. It burns, and Vincent is crying laughing by how striking they smell. We're not even aloud to have ranch or any dipping sauce to mellow out the spices. My we think of who in the world would think of such a cruel game to play. We're only three wings down. He puts his last wing down, stops and looks at me.

"Wow, how about we call it a draw and skip to some ice cream, deal?", Vincent says.

"Yes, I will completely second that. I expected them to be hot, but this is outrageous"

"I agree one thousand percent. I'm kind of like you now, I never felt this feeling before."

"Oh, so you enjoy prying on my innocence huh?"

He calls for the waiter, "Yes, can we get a bucket of strawberry ice cream sent to our table please."

"How did you know I liked strawberry?"

"Lucky guess, and by from your mouth impressions, I'd say you could take about anything cold to soothe your taste buds."

"Yeah except I don't have any left from this hot mess", I say with solace.

Mmmm. This ice-cream is way better than normal. I'm having fun talking to this Vincent guy. He draws my attention in nicely. Watching his eyes follow mine, and to see his interest tag along is beautiful like a sunny day. I wish I can stay here all day and listen to him pick my brain more. Having a guy do nice things for you, while you are both college students is promising. Maybe us women should stop holding a constitution over guys' head because of their age. Who said millennials can't rule the world. All it takes is effort and concentration on the power of love. Loving someone does not always mean in love or held over hills with a person. I could love someone's company, or I can love the way someone's words flow through my head because it is a pleasant feeling. It starts there. It begins with love. It is always weird to say that word, but it does not have to be. When you are filled with self- love, you almost want to spread it to others because the love is consuming and overflowing within you. But I won't say it to him. No, not just yet. I am aware he has lively thoughts, but it is just the first date, relax.

We wrapped it up and finish with a soul breaking "see you later" I understood it for what it was, nothing more. He left me with his number though, and that I can use it for whenever I am ready to let someone in because he could tell that I am still finding myself. How thoughtful of he to think of me first. I told him that be sure he is ready to listen when I come back from traveling my mind's mind a thousand miles away. He's a good guy, thank you God for a good guy.

I make it back home in time for work.

There's nothing no one can say to me that will ruin my day or this benevolent smile that's sitting upon my face. Everyone sees this attracting smile and wonders who put it there. It's none of there business rather. It isn't that I do not care for my coworkers, it's is that everybody gossips, and I am truly not a fan. I would rather keep busy with my work than talk about my feelings that neither one of them would too much care about. Talking out of turn is so simple and deconstructive. One day their all smiles and giggles and the next their calling out everyone in sight. I kind of question this way of communicating. How can you get aroused with such flawed theories? Why can't we all come to work and talk of such things like why the grass grows so tall, or even per say why is human nature evil. Conscious thinking is my forte. I like to open my mind's eye on days where I spend hours in one place. If I don't, then I become stagnant and lose my ability to become enlightened. Not that it is ever true, but I can become my environment the more that I procrastinate on vicious thoughts.

Customers come through and through and I make them feel comfortable in this environment. Many people do not like coming to the grocery store because it takes up too much of their time, so I make their visit relaxing as much as possible. However, others do find shopping therapeutic. If I only I knew the feeling. I'm always behind the counter, slicing meet, making sandwiches, and fixing hot plates for 20 hours a week. Although I am a college student, I wish I could receive at least 28 hours to help accommodate my expenses. No matter, this is only temporary. For now, I'll just pass through like a spirit climbing trees.

The clock strikes 7pm, and it's time to start breaking stations down and cleaning up. My station is the most complex, besides the cook's kitchen. I start pulling apart half of the sub-station and go to put my dishes in the sink. I make the water extra hot with a little of bleach to kill the dirt. I don't why I get so excited about this part. When it's time to start cleaning, I then know that is almost time to go home. While my dishes soak for a hot minute. I get out the water hoses in the back and flip the switch to wash. I run the hoses until the water heats up, and then I go to town on my side of the deli. In between cleaning, you must help customers with whatever they may need, so sometimes this part can keep you from clocking out on time. Over time is not recommended. However, you can't leave a station unkept, so the logical thing to do is clean until you are finished. Usually I have no trouble getting out on time, but that is just because my desire to go home highly influence my work ethic. I have kind of learn the ropes enough to know how the system works. If you work fast and complete your mini task, you will have no problem leaving when expected. If you walk around, twittle your fingers and wait 'til the store closes to do all of your dirty work, then of course you will be there until 11pm or midnight. I wash, rinse and sanitized the floor with the same hoes leaving the floor soaked and ready to be wiped away. I hurry to go get the squeegee. I do not need any interruptions while water is running over this floor. Workers will start to step back in forth in it, trailing food particles all across my station. A mess, no thank you. I began at on side and work my way down. The trick is getting all of the food they may have ran up under the tables from there. There's usually more than you think because you are cleaning from a mess that has been built up from an entire day of work. Welcome to night shift. Yes, okay finally, all the water is up and down the drain. It's 730, next is washing out the drain filled with food droppings. I grab a white bucket and fill it up with water, while I go grab some plastic gloves. I open the drain and wash all the food down the drain. Man, what a nice bill for the plumbers. Next task is to clear out

CAN YOU KEEP A SECRET?

half the hotline that has old or stale food in there. We know what is good from what is not by the times that they were put in there. The dirty dishes, this time, goes to the kitchen for the cook to clean. I just clean out the hot line with soap and water, once the dishes have been cleared from it.

830

9:00

One hour before closing, and before I get up out this store. I quickly go grab the soup buckets that we keep out in the beverage station and go wash them out. My feet are killing me by this point, and I'll feel it even more when I go and take a break.

"why would you go an take a break, you are almost about to leave", Leena said.

" I really do not think it is any of your business quite frankly, and plus all workers that have worked over six hours get at least a 10 minute break, according to the policy", I reply back.

She had nothing to say, but it's pure jealousy. The fact that I am nearly done with all of my work forty minutes before the store closes, yet she still has over an hour work of stuff to do.

CAN YOU KEEP A SECRET?

She's not liked by most anyway, as if I care. One thing I have learned with working in this store is that these elders would like their respect and don't mind forcing the promising idea upon you. Though, I think, how can someone tell me what to do or want such praised when we are in the same line of work. The only difference is this is not my career, this is my job. I respect you for your purpose, but don't think you can boss me around just because you are older. I chose a pathway, and you chose a grocery store, but let me just take my break and continue with my shift.

I come back inside and there isn't much for me to do. I have one last side of the sub bar to take down and I'm out of here. 9:45 hits and I throw out the rest of my bread, break the bar down and proceed with the dishes. Done. My last task for me to complete this work day, and I am out of here. Time to take out the trash. One of the produce guys always helps me out with this one because in his eyes a woman should not ever take out or throw out garbage in the bin. I thank him kindly for his respect and clocked out with joy.

Now I can reflect on my feelings for my lunch date properly. As I gather my things from the back, I say my respected goodbye even though the others are looking at me in disgust. They'll probably talk about me later, I laughed. This will not consume me because this isn't my life. This interaction at this store is just a moment in time.

On my way home, I play the latest jams from Jay-Z. My night is complete.

The Next Day

I decide to wake Vin with a good morning text. I know he wasn't expecting it, but my emotions would not let me do anything else. Plus I see him all the time on campus, so it feels right. He wants to meet for breakfast, but I decline on the account that I take too long to get ready in the mornings. If I had went, I would not have made it to class on time. He understood. I did let him walk me to class though, that was much of his favorite. Such a classic boy, I have no idea what to do with. He does this all of fall semester, and we go on quite the number of dates. He keeps me laughing and smiling all throughout the day. With this much excitement in my life, I think it's time he met my father. That will be the true test because if my dad does not like him, then I cannot and will not see him anymore. I have been through too much with my parents to not respect their opinion. Why not, it should not be all bad.

"I'm nervous, what if he doesn't like me.", Vin says.

CAN YOU KEEP A SECRET?

"Oh my gosh, can you not be much more of a class act.

"You adore me, so just let him see that through your eyes."

"What if my eyes are shut the entire time I am talking with him?"

I look at him in a dull way.

"Can you blame a guy? I didn't think I would even get this far by talking to you. My opinion was that you were too far out of my league. I mean tear droplets fell from my eyes every time you would walk into the gym. I couldn't stand to look at you too long because it literally hurt my eyes. I couldn't blink for nothing."

I shut him up with a kiss and ask, "now how do you feel?"

He blushes and says, "I felt nothing."

I decide to spruce is up a bit and put my tongue on top of his lip. while wrapping my lips around his for a tight kiss.

"How about now", I asked.

He smacks his lips amusingly. "You think you're slick now, but I already done got you now. What makes you think I'm nervous?"

I laughed in amazement, "babe, you said it, and plus you are talking way too fast for me to keep up."

"Well, let me go get my life together and at least pick out some nice clothes. When am I meeting him again?", he asks "Friday night before we go to the movies', I reply.

We stay up all night talking. I don't know why we do this, knowing that we have class every day of the week. It's something about our talks that I can't get enough of. The talks usually go with more of him talking and me listening. He's either giving me great advice on how I can move forward in life, or he is shaping his mind around the fact that he now has a woman in his life and all the means that come with it. We get off the phone early one night because I told him I wanted to spend time with my journal:

He thought it was cute that a girl my age would still even have one. I think that if I didn't I would surely go crazy. Sometimes journal my thoughts go that way anyway with you because you bring out my best emotions. This time I would like to talk about prosperity. Often, I forget my connection with nature, and that is my biggest fear. How can I move away from something that has been within me for so long? I may not can go to the beach everyday or live by it for that matter, but I can spend a great amount of time with her. I'll never forget the way

44

she looks at me. She has all the answers to my undiscovered questions. One day, I'll talk to her about my cycle to get a better understanding of what it means when she connects to me. I know, forever, she is with me. I just must know more about her. I would rather not get upset all the time when she comes to visit me. I wonder if she has the same cycle. How does she feel when her leaves depart, yet the sun never fries them when they return? She keeps her color, while the trees trace another circle around its trunk. How she might be opposite from her neighbors. She looks at me through a glass pane, and I see we have the same features. Her skin, my skin, it matches perfectly. If I could rest inside the trees somedays and just let the apples fall beside me, then I will complete our bondage by hugging her so tightly whether it's by smelling her everlasting scent that cannot be replicated, or me sitting under a tree and crying my eyes out until her roots start to spread beneath my feet. Either way, I don't want to come across her as selfish. Though how can I give back to her to let her know I am present in her awareness. It still baffles me journal, but I want growth and prosperity. I can walk for miles on solid ground trying to find my resemblance within her limbs. I won't know my difference unless I eat from her or grow my own. I can connect to my inner verse. I won't stop until she knows how beautiful she is without looking in the mirror. Goodnight journal, thanks for listening.

Friday

Friday comes and I'm so excited. Not so much for the date, but for a new beginning I am giving myself with trusting in the worlds of nature. Every word used to describe her, I project back to others. There it is, that's how I will give. Vin walks me to class, gives me a tight hug, and whispers in my ear that everything will fall into place before your soul captures a striking disarray. How did he know what I was feeling? I never spoke of my insecurities to him. It's not like it shows weakness. I decided not to share so much of my personal intuition with him before I knew who I was. She's talking to him without my permission. Before I get too creeped out I shake my head astonished and go into my classroom.

I'm so distracted. My mind's eye is focusing on every detail the professor is saying. Flipping words in different orders, changing the way they sound when you put them together, my how she's coming into form before my eyes. I stop to ask the teacher a question to help follow along and make sure I am hearing him correctly. I am, and his answer was more than clear. I decide to stop looking for answers in the words that he is portraying and instead create my own definition of them. It makes a turnaround, these adjusted words. Compromising the concepts, I take notes. One thing I like about college is that you get real life conclusions with the graphic teachings, and I am sitting here absorbing it all. I take a sip of water to penetrate my thoughts. He starts a conversation that attracts my interest, race. He said it wouldn't be such of an issue if we all just stopped talking about it and that it conforms our mind into missing the bigger picture, so I asked him what is the greater good?

"It is not necessarily the greater good that we are aiming for, but the turbulent of human nature. We speak of human nature as if it does not exist. One race over the next exemplifies the power within us all, yet it is rusting in the near peaks of the wind. Is it that the simplicity of race is stopping us from being ever conjoined?', he ask.

I respond with, "It isn't that race is being simplified. We may not see color, but you can see the difference. The appearance of a body matches whether I am threatened. Am I threatened by my own race? Maybe so. Every race has an underlying factor that keeps us grounded. Fear. We naturally have this frame work from birth, so the "greater good" is without question another simplified term that cannot be distributed. My question for you sir, without disrespect, serpent, she, sword with your words you might be because of your authority, what makes one race greater than the next?"

"The resources", he replied

"And that professor is why we cannot unify our sanctuaries. We are all in this institution to grow and develop our mind's eye, yet we are captivated from these 'resources' because of financial aid and personal preferences. What takes us out of this realm?"

"Nature", he replies.

"Thank you. That was the rooted answer I wanted to hear. We are disconnecting from it so much it's sad to bear. So what of your color or not, nothing beats the strength of nature itself. That is why we build on top of it instead of within. With it wearing its face all around us, we still cannot look at it. Why? We're consumed with the bugs, dirt, and the scorching heat, and the cold winters, that it becomes just seasons to us. Okay, so how do we get better you asked? I don't know, I haven't figured that part out yet. I can't be the only one though that is helplessly tracing our ancestors' passion."

CAN YOU KEEP A SECRET?

"So if we're white, do we have ancestry?", a classmate asked.

"Your question defeats the topic. Great discussion today, class dismissed", the professor replies.

I can see the student's question was sincere, but the professor was right. We were getting away from naming it with melanin or without and more so on the history. I would justify and say some students will completely miss the point, but then I would be talking of myself as well because I have gotten away from what used to be so simple as to walking outside to observe the birds. I can't blame her for wondering. I often wonder too, sometimes if it all is even real or not. I won't get too depressed on it, I'll move forward from now with the impression that I can do better. I can think better. I am my own prosperous adventure. Vin waits for me outside the building.

"How was class?"

"Let's just say, I think I came to a discovery of my opinion."

"Finding yourself, right? What was that experience like?"

CAN YOU KEEP A SECRET?

"I can't put it into words just yet. I just know my heart stimulates for the mystery of a young woman like myself. You want to go grab some coffee on me?"

"Oh you're paying now? I'm not use to that."

"So don't get use to it, c'mon we're taking your car"

He looks at me and shakes his head, "You are something else my dear."

The coffee shop is amazing and simple with a balcony that you can oversee the cars strolling by.

It's still much too cold to sit out there. We make it formal and sit in chairs across from each other. The cool thing about this coffee place is that it does not have tables, so it makes the conversations personal to get into. I love it. For a while we are just sitting and chatting about much of nothing. Then, as he always likes to do, he throws a strategic question my way.

" Why do you think people choose to smoke weed?"

I take a sip of my coffee, "I think people like to be influenced. Why do you think we have commercials? Movies? Sitcoms? We like for someone to take care of us naturally. When you are under the influence you are doing little to no work with your body. The marijuana or the alcohol is doing all of the work, so you can just "relax." Is that saying that we're lazy, no. It is the simple concept of less stress that we put onto our body when thinking of the next assignment, or when the next pay period will be. I would not say we smoke to forget. Most say we do it to become more enlightened, but neither one is true. How can you become enlightened to something you know nothing about? Knowledge just does not pop out of thin air. Of course, when under we like to ask specific questions to find more about what us is inside. Though who is answering those questions? A friend whom is also high? I'm not speaking from existence, I am speaking from experience. It isn't until you come down from your high that you begin questioning things because of how increased your senses were. So you're saying the more your senses are heightened, the more you inquire about the world around you and draw your own conclusions? No. Are you really smarter, when you are letting someone or something do all of your thinking for you. When it's over and you are all out, you are still back to your same routine. Didn't stop to make a difference in the world, just expected to blend in and speak of senseless observations. Well then I'd say that we are selfish because in my optic alignment human nature is balanced. We like to find ways to tip the spectrum, but it comes back to equality when we're done throwing the stone. We see things to get inspired. To empower our mind's eye, we think we must elevate to it in a way that is uncommon. How does marijuana differ? If someone walked up to you and said that they would wash all your worries away with just one strand, you maybe wouldn't trust it, but you would consider it. You might even question your own instinct because of its raves reviews. At the end of the day if you don't know self, than what are you really reviewing. I can pick a leaf off a tree, skin it or maybe even brew it, mix it in some hot water to make tea and it could very well give me the same effect. Who wouldn't want to smoke a joint or drink some hot tea that would calm your nerves after a long day? It's the ideal principle that you have will to keep in mind of the side effects. It's so popular and is a hit because people rather put their problems into one sense of being. Even if you do not have problems that you are dealing with, it gives you that extra push to do something great. Think about it, on any substance, why do you think people talk so much? It's not always a cry for help, but your body and mind is calling out for something. Sure marijuana is a plant that is grown from ground up, but why touch it if you didn't grow it yourself. Many hands and auras pass through these strands, so it is tainted by the time it reaches your hands. Is it powerful enough to change form from being in a place of someone else? It's not what it used to be they say.

He breaks in, "Well of course not. Back then the soil wasn't disrupted. If the plant grew, it grew naturally. It may have well been stronger than what we see today. I don't trust the hands of others, so I always bless it before rolling it.

We both laugh.

"Bless the man's grace", I say.

"What brought upon your enthusiastic charisma for the things and aspects of our near world.", he asks.

"Well why wouldn't I be keen to the rhythm of the bird. It's logical to want to embrace what I was born with."

"But you've quoted our essence is a blank slate."

"Also, true. Though we do adapt to what is here now, so why not question where it came from?"

Our conversation would continue for centuries if I had not reminded him of our plans tonight. It was a great date none the less. I know that when we are together it is mostly filled with

CAN YOU KEEP A SECRET?

dispersing energy and knowledge, but how else do you get to know a person. It's prominent that I know where his head is at before I know anything else. I like that he lets me do all the talking though. Sometimes I do it too much. He asks the right questions, so I know he is following along. Anyway, we're going to see Black Panther tonight, so I hope he's ready for my dad.

At Home

"Hey dad he's on the way, stick it to him good when he gets here.."

I go and get dress. I would wear a dress, but it's spring, which means the wind is still blowing. I'm not about to freeze trying to look cute. It's a cultured film, so I decide to dress for the occasion. I search for a long sleeve printed shirt with printed pants. No matter if the prints match up, I like the definition of the fabric. I decide to tie a blazer around my waist to set it off. The door bell rings. I run to the bathroom to finish my look, makeup. I can hear dad inviting him in. I crack the door just a little bit to over hear what they are talking about. Me, of course, but ssh let's listen.

"So start with your name, your full name, and then your age", dad says.

"Vincent Gilbert the 2nd, and I am 22 with a birthday of April the 9th."

"So, tell me about yourself, I can figure out the rest by looking you up in the system."

CAN YOU KEEP A SECRET?

I laugh out loud. Oh, my goodness, what is this a job interview? Dad is unbelievably corny. If I listen anymore they'll over here me. I close the door and finish the rest of my face. The quicker I do my face, the more I can save Vin from dad's inspector gadget investigation.

I walk out,

"All done", I say loudly.

They look at me as if the sun just broke through the ceiling.

"What are you wearing", dad says.

"Dad give it a rest, you'll never be able to wrap your head around my style. Plus we're going for the culture."

He whispers something under his breath. Vincent laughs. Whatever.

I signal dad the thumbs up and he returned the favor. Great! Dad likes him, and now we can go. This is so weird.

We get in the car and drive off. I tell him to drive slow at first, so it doesn't seem out of the ordinary. He's so shaken up, he is driving below 20mph. I check the speedometer. He looks at me.

"I'm sorry, I'm just nervous"

"The questioning is over, relax. He likes you,"

He blushes, "What makes you so sure."

"I'm his daughter. Look we're past the house. Can you just drive now."

He drives off, and we make it to the movies just in time before the lights go down.

"I can't believe you almost made us late to the showing", I whisper to him.

"You were the one with your fancy style that no one can understand."

"Ssh it's starting."

"Woah that was good, we must see that again", I say.

"You mean right now?"

"What is with you tonight, you can't seem to compreh..'

"It was a joke babe. My do you have to be so political all of the time."

"So what do you think was the message behind it?", I asked

"Well what wasn't. I mean it was sick. I think it was one of those movies that was good for the soul. I mean it's evolutionary seeing a black superhero for the first time in what like ever? There was no wrong throughout the story line. Everybody had a reason for caring out an action that seemed unfit. Even when the king switch persons, you still went along with the new king because of his dominance. It lures you in to believe that he deserves his position. You didn't necessarily think that he was wrong for being king because of what they did to him. He had his way of life taken from him before he could even have a choice into what he wanted to do with it. I think you must watch the movie more than once to find the significance. I won't say the story was too fast, but I do wish it would have been longer. The introduction was too quick for me. I forgot why the metal held such weight in the movie because of it. I loved it though. I'm not a script writer, so I can't critic it intellectually."

Fast Forward.

A summer's day and we took a drive down Lover's Lane. It was this long road of voluptuous trees and mosey drapings where there was nothing but land all around us. A couple houses here and there; nowhere close to the road though. Therefore, it made it seem like it was our own road, our own city, our own business. How great it felt to just talk with the windows down and laugh with no one else on the road. It was a long road, lover's lane. Our destination was the city's closest park. Riding there would bring every conversation either one of us could ever talk about. The same thoughts every day and they were all from him. Amazing how someone can change your mind like that. I remember my teacher in public speaking would always say, "when you give a persuasive speech, no matter if you change their mind a centipede down the spectrum, you still changed some form of your audience way of thinking" Applying that to my love life, man what a speech. That is nor here nor there. Maybe later it will make sense. Him and I would ride down lovers lane absorbing a little tree and elevating our mind all of the time. This time was different, however. He stimulates my senses. It was like he was making love to me with his words. Every syllable running together into the tone of his voice, made me shiver. Every time he would glimpse over here to end his point and meet with my eyes, my back would relax. It was like floating on his words, as he was dancing deep inside. I felt it deep in my stomach, and it felt like butterfly kisses. I started to value him as a King. I put his needs before mine.

Edgewater, so seamless. I got all excited because it was a different kind of date. Though all of our dates have been out the ordinary. I thought the best way to enjoy something was to feel it with your skin. I took my shoes off to feel what it felt like to sink. The grass was ever so soft and green, I wanted my body to consume its comfort. Let me sleep in it. Instead, I just got on a bended knee and got a whiff of what God produces on a daily basis. I knew it seemed awkward to just stop all of a sudden and smell the grass. I looked back up at him, and he just smiled. "What does it smell like", he asked. Wow, he's interested. I blushed and said fresh love. You know the love that you get in abundance, but don't know where it came from. It just fills your nose and you can't stop nor change the feeling. Yeah, kind of like that. He was speechless, yet admired my senses. He told me that if the grass smelled that good, then he must touch it himself. He began taking his shoes off and I kind of started to giggle. I guess we will land here.

He pulled out the blankets, and I gathered the basket.

"Babe, take everything out, including the drinks" I knew he wasn't going to forget the drinks.

"Where you going", he asked.

"Oh I just have to feel the water." I step down the hill, and I walk a little further. It was like I was looking at a small ocean, watching the ripples flow back and forth. I take one more step and I can now feel the water streaming against my toes. He walks over to me.

"So what does that feel like"

"I can't explain it", I begin to say. "It's as almost as if the water is humming."

"Well, if water could talk, then what would it say?"

"I'm not sure it is an 'it' per say. Maybe she's trying to tell me something. I don't know. Perhaps we should fill our belly and sip on some booze. Maybe that will loosen my senses.

Babe and I start to eat the classic peanut butter and jelly sandwiches. We're laughing and spreading words of joy.

"So what is it with you and nature for you to feel so connected to it", he asked.

" I don't know really. I just know that whenever I'm around her, I get this tingly feeling inside as if I am suppose to do something."

" Do something with her? For her? What is it that you must do?", he replied.

I laugh, "I'm not sure yet babe, that is what I must know." What I am aware now is that I am tipsy. I figure this is the perfect time for me to go touch her hand again.

"Babe, come with me to the water. Maybe you can feel it too."

"Sorry Jah, I don't mean to laugh, but…Okay if that is what you feel than maybe I can feel it as well." We walk down to the wet grass.

"Don't rush it, let the water come to you", I suggest. He looks at me and smile.

"You really love this don't you"

"She's my best friend. Oh wait shh, here she comes." The ripples slowly approach our toes and she was so cooling, I crotched down until I was lying flat beside her.

"Okay babe, you have on clothes, so you will get soaked."

"I want to, I have to know her story." I'm looking upside down at him and he shakes his head with a smile. He gets low and kisses my forehead and whispers, "just don't go too far."

I move an inch over more so my body is now in the water. Watching the clouds disperse into nothing, while my body shifts with the water. I'm floating. I'm creating images in my mind, but it looks as if they are coming to life bouncing through the clouds. I feel the humming sensation again, maybe I should swim back. I put my arms under water, and my head starts to fall. I sink and let her gravity take over my body. That tingling sensation has came back to my body. I start to swim. Through the vines I go and deeper my mind sinks. I see a dark shadow in the water. I look to each side of me and there's nothing there. How can it be, when the shadows are closing in. I've been under too long, so I come up for air with a big gasping sound.

"JAH, ARE YOU OKAY?", babe shouted.

"I think so. The water feels nice." I started to float my way back. The sun is beaming on my face, so I close my eyes and let the water take me. It feels nice here.

"Come to me, the water is great today."

"Babe, you know I can't swim."

"Just stick your feet in, I want you to feel this synergy."

"Okay I'm coming babe."

He takes off his shoes and slowly walks down to the bank.

"Okay, now what", he asked.

"Ahahaha can't you just enjoy her beauty sweetheart?"

He looks at me funny, and makes little splashes with his toes. How adorable.

"How does it feel honey? Can you feel her sensations?"

"…."

I know what that look means. I swim back and he gets up to return back to our spot. I lay my towel beside his and I spread my arms and legs out wide, so the sun can glorify my skin.

"Aren't you hungry babe?"

"I am, but I like this feeling right here in this moment. It's quiet."

"So you want me to be quiet too?", he asked.

CAN YOU KEEP A SECRET?

"Please."

He starts to pull out a bag of Doritos, and I gaze over at him in the corner of my eye.

"Can I not eat?"

I shut my eyes and smile. Five minutes pass and my body absorbs the heat. My mind is traveling through the liquor and I soon begin to fall asleep. I over here babe dust off his hands and put away the chips. I can feel his breath on my shoulder, but I don't speak. I hear him pull out something, but I can't make out what it is just yet. I hear the lid open. He starts to rub his hands together and immediately I can figure he is putting on lotion. Then all of a sudden he puts his hands on my thighs. "Oh its oil." His hands felt warm against my skin, and the oil made it very easy for his fingers to seep into my skin.

"Thank you", I utter.

He has a tight grip on my leg, as he's twisting it in circles. His hands so smooth going against my skin, as the sun melts the tension within my legs. Now he makes his way down to my feet; the best part. He rubs his knuckle into my sole, squeezes my foot with both hands, and twist and turn as he goes up and down the sides of my feet. My feet make like drums as he pounds and beats them up. I get these massages more often then necessary. With his hands though, I always find some necessary excuse to be touch by them. I feel the vibration now that he is finish. It is a tingly energy that is running through the veins in my feet. They are completely numb, and I'm afraid to get up. Before I can even toss over to get even more comfortable, I'm awaken with,

" I know you're hungry."

Well indeed I was, but then again when am I not ever hungry. I sit up and look next to me with a smile. I lean in for a kiss, but he backs away saying jokingly, "babe, you have morning breath." I laugh and grab my kiss myself. He's so sweet, I think to myself as he fixes my lunch plate. He smacks his lips a little bit and says,

"So did she have any words for you today."

"Not today, she showed face with her shadows, but that was as close as I could get to her."

"Do you think she is afraid of you"

"Well, I would never have guess, but why would she be?"

"Well you know nature's way of speaking to the unknown is giving her something to break through."

"Since when did you become an expert of her more than me. I'm the woman, shouldn't I know more?"

"Well of course nature would come to you first, but us men can observe better who you women are actually. You guys speak the loudest when you are most vulnerable.

I smiled.

We talk some more of nature's best reactions. His words are so soft spoken. We turn over on our sides and stare at each other for a moment. Many smiles and giggles are shared. I can see why I chose him. His mind is a delicate fruit, and his body is poised with symmetry.

He says, "I know this is a common question, but from your perspective, how do you view love?"

"Well for starters there are many love languages to love that I believe many people skip over when they fall. More than often lovers do not view love they crave it. It is as if they cannot see, while they are walking."

"Are we supposed to view it before we choose who we want to be with", he asked.

"Define 'view'."

CAN YOU KEEP A SECRET?

"Well, how do we know what we are receiving if we cannot recognize it. My definition of a viewpoint is leveling up your mind to the point where you can see the beauty of love. How do we see this view in a woman without mistaking it for something else? A lot of people will say you will feel it first, but we all know and then that this statement is not all the way valid. Feeling a woman's beauty is mystic."

"I believe you are to let it come to you in the mist of air. Some people search for this view, but the view is way better when nature shows you first. She comes in many shapes, so you''ll never know it's completely her. It is like going up a skyscraper for the first time and looking out unto the distance. You don't know what you will see because it is your first time looking at it from this angle. Though once you come into her presence, she makes herself known by applying her gift to your senses. It happens at once. It feels like a burst of new energy or as soft as a dandelion. Very fragile she is, yes I know, but that's my perception of the view.

We get home from a long day out in the sun, and I immediately head for the shower. I take a peak to see what Vin is doing on the way by, and he is preparing food in the kitchen. Ugh, wow, more food, just for me. How sweet. I hope it's my favorite tonight. I hurry up to the bedroom to prepare for my shower, and I begin to think that I wouldn't want nothing more than to sit in the jacuzzi. I know, I know, I must wash first, so I do. The shower is steaming on my back just how I like it. Going around my body with this soft exfoliating soap, reminding myself of the day's beauty inside of the water. Of course, in the shower it feels different. There's no roots or trees around. Our water comes from a well though. It's water, it's her, she's here soaking her decorations beneath my skin. One wash at a time, as I take my rag up and down my shoulder, round about on my legs, and between my small stomach rolls. I sigh a long deep breath of relief and cut the shower off. Taking my towel off the rack, I go on over to the jacuzzi and start the jets.

Vin takes a peak through the double doors, "You know the longer you stay in the water, the more your skin will have its own ripple."

"Wow, did you think of that joke all yourself?"

"Yes"

"It just feels so good babe, almost like the ocean itself."

CAN YOU KEEP A SECRET?

"Yeah right, I'll be back."

"What does he know, he's a guy", I think to myself.

This time the water is extra...I think I'll just relax until the food is ready.

I walk downstairs into the living room, and I look around in awe.

He walks towards me for a hug..

"No candles, rose petals on the floor or in scent?"

He turns around and walks back to the kitchen.

"Hahaaha babe, it's just jokes. Our house feels lovely without a view...get it?"

"How was your swim?", he says to me.

"Very funny. I do have a strong appetite though. What's to eat?"

One of my favorites, hot wings.

This is great babe, no really. Thanks for cooking up trouble.

"Oh the game's on", he saids.

" 'Oh the game's on', as if you didn't set this up perfectly."

"Babe, you love the game."

"Yeah when I'm drunk"

"I can fix that"

He brings out the goods, Tequila GOLD.

"Oh, you sure you just want to watch the game?"

"Yes, babe no doubt about it."

Oh well damn, no wink, no kiss with it. I guess he's serious. Shut me all the way down then. He aligns the shot glasses up, there's at least about ten in a row.

"He's trying to have me on my ass", I whisper.

"Okay babe, so just like every other time when we watch the game, every commercial take two shots."

I just smile and curse him out in my head. I don't know why I always agree to this. None the less though, it is quite a fun game we play. Here we go.

Drinks start pouring commercial after commercial. At this point I don't really care who wins, I just want both games to be over and we are only on shot number six..out of ten.

CAN YOU KEEP A SECRET?

Vin's moving up and down from the couch depending on
who's kicking the field goal and what not. Sitting across from
me, he starts giving me his soft eyes. I already knew what time
it was, but the game was not over yet. I knew he would not
leave that spot under any circumstances. I got up, went to the
kitchen to get another wing and sat back down. I ate it with a
look on my face. He saw that I was acting impatient, so he went
in and kiss my forehead, my cheek, and stopping at my lips. I
guess it doesn't hurt to smile. Uh oh, here goes another
commercial. I paused after the seventh shot. I thought my next
move was to head for the bathroom, so I paused for a sec. One
minute I'm in tuned, and in visioning the game as real life, and
the next I'm back in human reality. Vin's the head of the blue
team, while I am head of the green, in my mind. I see some
players run into each other and I get weak. It feels like sex. One
of blue's players takes the ball and runs to the end goal. I'm
thinking soon as he touch, another rotation in the world has
come. Time to get up again. I walk to the kitchen. I'm moving
around and my arm starts to tremble. It's probably nothing, I
think. Though when I go to reach for something, it slips
between my fingers. What an odd feeling. I reach for the

refrigerator with my left hand again, and I have no strength. I reach for it with my right hand. "Okay, so I haven't totally lost it." I grab a water and head back for the couch. Another commercial, and I'm three shots behind. I reach for one.

"Babe, it's okay. You can stop here."

"Thank you", I reply.

I slump back on the couch. Finally, half time.

"How you feelin slim dog."

"After those shots babe, I don't think I am slim anymore."

"Can I kiss you", he said.

"Where."

"Where can I start?"

"My legs."

So he does. Just up and down hitting my pressure points with his thumb and fore fingers, while gently pressing his lips into my skin.

"After the game, you want to light up?"

"Lol babe, you make it sound as if we are playing", I said oddly after reminding myself of her thoughts.

"Sure, my love. Anything with you is always a trip."

CAN YOU KEEP A SECRET?

The game's back on, and it is happening again. I can't fathom what I'm thinking. I try to sleep for the rest of the game. I can't. My mind is racing, and my heart is literally skipping beats. One minute I'm falling into ever land, and my back hits this brick making this pounding inside my head. I toss back over. I am jumping off a roof with nothing to protect my fall. A tear starts to roll down the side of my eye. Is it her? My eyes open. I sit up.

"Babe, what's the matter. Did I do something wrong? Here let me make you some tea.", he says.

"I don't know, maybe it was just a dream."

"I know you don't want to share, do you?"

"I'm sorry, but no, I wouldn't."

"Here I tell you what me dahlin, let's go unto the back porch and smoke a spliff just to calm your nerves, nothing more nothing less."

We sit face to face on the couch, while he is on one side and I'm on the other. I volunteered to roll. He passes me the rolling papers. I take one long one out and begin. Thinking to myself, " I deserve this. I am worthy of her company." With every tuck and push, I think again that this is how our world is chanting. Every feeling and movement now resembles how we live. Any move I make, my footprint has left some mark somewhere in the world. I light up slowly and watch the paper fold back. After two rotations, I begin to feel the juice and the herb. My body is humming and my spirit is no longer there. With this tug hitting my mind, I rest my head against his shoulder. I'm dreaming again. This time, I'm taking everyone up into the new love Vin and I have created. I stand on top of earth looking down at the waters, and I see the ones who don't know the secret. They're struggling, so I reach down and grab one person at a time. Each time he/she lands, there is a gold ring that flares around earth. All our friends down there unawaken…we're going to need more help.

I awake and out of touch with what Vincent is saying. I scooch closer to him as he sits on the edge of the chair as I press my shoulder against his just to see if I can hear him any better. He must be speaking in code, since he must know that our time here is running low. Catching little fragments here and there, I put together sentences of the complete opposite in my head to make up what he is saying. I squint my eyes in frustration. Inside I shout, SPEAK TO ME, I CAN'T HEAR ANYTHING

CAN YOU KEEP A SECRET?

YOU ARE SAYING." This rush stops and starts at different parts of his sentences. I slam my head into my hands, and I stay there with tears coming down my eyes. I over hear him trying to figure out what's wrong, calling my name, wiping my tears. This is nothing of the norm. I go inside to lie down.

My body couldn't pull itself together to lie on the bed, so I sat in our room and waited. Overhearing him say something, once again I could not make out. Maybe he was on the phone. I don't know. My nerves were not calm at all, they were shot. It might help, if I sip a little bit more of this brown, so I took one last shot of Tequila and I'm there. Completely out of mind I am, but I do not feel disoriented anymore. Maybe it was my nerves. He walks in and I start smiling and laughing. He smiles and asks me what's so funny. I reply with "nothing" and that I am just feeling good. Vin looks confused for a second.

"But you had tears, and was mumbling words I could not understand out there. Babe I'm concerned. Are you positive absolutely sure that there is nothing wrong."

I pull the covers off me and ask him does there look as if anything is wrong.

CAN YOU KEEP A SECRET?

He flashes a smirk and walks his hands to the side of me. Putting one foot onto the bed, he begins to take off his shirt. I'm gazing as he lifts it up, and I watch the chocolate appear from every corner. His natural smell fills my nose as I go in to help him finish. The buckle is next, and I take my time with this one. "No mess ups", I'm thinking. One hook after the next, and I head for the zipper. I tell him to lie down. I kneel next to his waist, and grabbed some oil. I rubbed my hands tightly together to make the oil warm as I go in to massage his abdomen.

"Let me heat you up", I say.

To get him aroused, I place my tongue on him and massage it around. First his tip, and then I slip my way down. I began moaning so he could feel a little sinful. It soon got messy with me slurping and using my hands. I had enough. I get up and squat over him. Tonight, I'm his dancer. I slowly went down and my peach started dripping. He slowly pumped his way through. He connected. A rush it was. I'm bouncing. Slowly turning my hips from side to side, with my eyes close. The liquor's starting to move, and I begin dreaming. I drift up to the solid white clouds. I'm above. Looking out, I see nothing below. We've reached bliss: The promise land. I began walking through heaven's trail trying to stay afloat. With bricks and pot holes in the road it's hard to balance. I sink back down and ride his waist back and forth. He hit that sweet spot and I came face to face with God, except he didn't have a face. I felt the trees shaking, the grass waving, the pebbles rising, and the water rippling. We were there. Standing in front of the glass gates, I waited for them to be open. I heard tiny crystals rubbing together as they began to open. We couldn't move our feet to go in. It wasn't our time. We had to go back down and finish what we have started. Now we're in the woods together. My mind drops a little deeper, so I go in close to his chest. I commence kissing his neck, shoulder, face. With every kiss, I walk a step further on the trail. We were barefooted, so we felt every grain of sand run between our toes. I look around and I see figures in the mix of the trees and their whispering "love" repeatedly. I don't recognize the silhouettes at first. I think "maybe it's nothing." However, their rhythm is turning me on. My head becomes foggy and every feeling turns numb. He bumped that spot again and instantly my body moves to the sway of his. I hear the chant again and kiss his lips to the sound of it. How I picture what the world would look like if we show them our love…a spiritual love. I take that as the reason we were turned around from the gates. The world needed love and maybe some real love at that. Something they can gravitate towards and spin around in a circle for. I wake up and stare into his eyes thinking he had felt all what I had dreamt. 5 seconds, 10 seconds go by and I break the stare. I lifted and lie next to him.

"Did you feel that", he said. "yes, I wasn't sure if it was real" "Oh it was real, feel in between your legs", he said. I did and started laughing. He got up to go get a towel and I'm thinking, "So we're suppose to change the world…with love." He comes back, wipes me down, and then proceeds to clean himself off. I got up, slipped on my clothes and left him with a kiss on the lips. "Thanks love." "For what", he whispers. "For making love to me."

He heads back outside to light one last spliff.

Moments later, Vin enters along with everyone else. While they're sitting and talking, I'm laying with a racing mind. This is not the same world I abandoned before my husband and I had sex. I over hear the guys talk about the game and how this pass should've been intercepted by this player. Well, how I should have done things a little different. Maybe I shouldn't have left

company like that. Next, they say something humorous but I'm
the only one laughing. Vin over heard my laughter and deeply
said "Go to Bed", so I thought. So stern he is now, wow where
did that come from. He must know. He must know I'm
pregnant. That is the only way I'm feeling everybody's energy
at once. We just created another life. The world's turning. My
head's spinning, and everything just keeps going up. God has
came, and I can't keep up. All of a sudden I think I'm sleeping,
and I hear the rain pour. I turn over to get a good glimpse, and it
is. It is raining. I slowly turn back to lie down. Soon as my head
cuffed the pillow, the rain stopped. Boom. Woah God, what are
you showing me. It must be a full moon. I hear the guys go
outside. Even though they were nowhere near the window, their
voices still lingered on. I tossed and turn. Hearing every word, I
added my own spin to it. I wasn't sleeping, and this isn't helpful
to the baby. He finally came to bed. I knew some hours had to
at least past because everyone was now at home. He lies down
and at first he was faces the opposite way. Maybe he was mad
at me. Soon after, he turned to face me and he brings me in
close. His covering is so tight, I like it.

I wake up the next day, thank God. All of those images in my head, I didn't know what I was seeing or what I was hearing. Did we throw a party last night, or was there another world inside of my head. All that mattered though was that my man was there. I go out into the living room and fifteen shot glasses were in the sink. Well…alright. Who knows what realm we went to last night, or was it just me? I didn't bothered asking. Keeping it inside really meant something to me. What would it matter for another opinion to form. Prancing around the house because I am the queen of it, I asked one of Vincent's friend if they could get me some toilet paper. I giggled inside. Watching him go get it, I thought, "I really am queen." He brought it back to me and all I could think of was love. Well, maybe if I thank him with my eyes he'll get the picture. To me, it was harmless. I was expressing my gratitude in a different way. He just needed to think about it to know how to accept it. I took the toilet paper and softly uttered a thank you. Sitting on the toilet, my mind flips again. Every time I relieve myself, I send all of those negative opinions down the drain. Whomever thinking whatever really doesn't matter because my intentions is always love. I made a promise to God during our sensual sin that I would show love, so that it shall be. The day went by and the night fell. That's when these shadows really come out to play.

His mom comes over with food and I spring up. I thanked her and went to the living room. Eating, I could feel my belly growing. I know it's early, but there is a feeling of another energy inside of me. I know I'm pregnant. I know it's true. Vin's brother then comes over. One person after the next and I couldn't take it. I immediately shouted for wine. I shouted at his friend to go fetch me some and he looked at me strange. I was the queen though, and this is my castle. What I want goes. What I say matters. No one would give me any… Constantly yelling and seeing no one respond, I went over to his brother and grabbed for his head. I slam it against the wall. He drifts back. His older brother steps in and tries to fight me off but I pulled against him. He's holding me up now, begging me to stop at once. I scratch his arms until I see blood and the paleness of his flesh. It satisfies me. I try to break his grip by pushing and pulling further away from him until he got me to the ground. "J, LET GO." "LET GO NOW!." I see Vincent enter from the back. My love. It looks as if he just finished a hot shower. His body is steaming, and not to mention, but so is his head. He's on fire. "WHAT THE HELL IS GOING ON", he shouts. I take glimpses around to see everybody crying and shouting. Someone whispered, "I think we should call the police." I shouted back for them to be call this instance. I didn't know what I was saying, It just felt right. My mind shut out from all sounds, so I did not even hear the knock at the door. The police rushed over along with some paramedics. I heard that one last "let go", and I fell to the ground. With my legs spread out and my arms wide, I laid there. Everybody is looking hazy, and I see my spirit come to sit beside me.

"Jah don't fail me now. You still must complete the mission, no matter of whom you're in love with", she said.

I can't focus on the rest of her words. What was she saying, what does all of this mean. I can't take it anymore. I let out a strong cry and yell for everyone to stop touching me, but no one was.

By that time, the lights were out. Hearing voices speaking to me, I listen to none.

"Mam, are you okay?" "May I have your name mam?" Then a flashlight came over me and I was someone else. I

looked at the police and he said, "Mam can you sit up for me?"
I thought I was going to jail. I was ready though. All the stuff
they did to me, I was ready for war. Fighting to hold back, a tear
fell and I cried out, "You..killed... my people." With my fist
pressing hard into the ground, I said it once again. One last
"Mam can you sit up for me" and I flashed back. Vincent was
sitting right there on the couch, waiting for me to rise. I look at
him and the others. He's in tears, but I feel no remorse.

"You did this to me", I cried.

I didn't know who he was. I mean I knew who he was to
me, but I wasn't sure if all that was true anymore.

"Mam, is your name Jahanna Gilbert?"

Who…

Chapter 8

I don't know how I got into the ambulance, but I rode. As I'm riding, the car is twisting and turning. I didn't know where I was going. I was no longer on earth. Maybe I wasn't dreaming. I thought I completed my mission, and he was taking me to the promise land. Anywhere I go, I am queen of love, so I'm not even listening or paying attention to where we're going. Two people appear on the side of me.

"Where the hell did you guys come from?"

"We've been here the whole time mam, watching you whisper small things to yourself. You are not well mam. Have you taken anything tonight?

"A shot of love, now leave me alone unless you want to be six feet under."

It's taking forever to get to where ever it was that I "must go at once."

I fall asleep slowly into another dream. Why am I having all of these dreams? They are shaking me and turning me upside down. I fight back. I slam my fist down and the medics wake me.

"Mam, please try to stay awake. We can't lose you, you are very important to us"

I knew it! They did too! This is a complete set up and I am right about everything, except for where we are going. Damn it. They'll be hearing from my lawyer soon. As if I even have one, but they did kidnap me and I must take this to the courts. Is it too late for prayer?

We arrived. I was put into a rolling chair, and wheeled up into a tall slender building. I didn't see which it was. They were rolling me too fast. What is the big deal anyway? I didn't do anything wrong. I just demanded my respect in my own damn house. What's a woman have to do around here to be perceived as dominant. A man's world right, and I'm just living it. All the time, answering to a man, and paying bills to the man. There stopping me from being great. I'm tired. It's time for a revolution.

CAN YOU KEEP A SECRET?

It didn't occur to me that I was in the hospital until they asked for a urine sample. I thought this was it. This was the moment they were going to validate my pregnancy. I took the test and went back to this small waiting room. There was only one chair in such small space. A room for myself, yeah they know who I am. I opened the door.

"Um excuse me, nurse, am I pregnant?"

"Well, what do you think honey", she replied.

I smiled and closed the door. I knew it! However, one baby was not causing all this raucous inside of me. I soon grew tired of waiting, so I lift the seat's handle to go back. I flipped and turned around in this medical chair, and my head was doing the same. Someone walked in and it was him, my husband. He held my face and looked into my eyes. I looked back at him and said,

"babe we're expecting."

"What are you talking about?"

"Honey, we are having a baby. I think it's a little girl."

He minds nothing of what I'm saying. He just looks at me and smiles with a "Okay baby." My mom walked in and he walked out. Worried as ever, she looked at me and said,

CAN YOU KEEP A SECRET?

"What's going on Jahanna? Why are you here."

I gladly smiled and said that I was having a baby. The look on her face was very much disturbing. I knew she wasn't ready for a little one yet. This was my choice. My life. When were people going to start caring for me. I don't remember the rest of our conversation, but I'm sure she left the room in utter distraught. I could hear her fussing to Vincent from behind the door. He had no words for her either, and I'm pretty sure he doesn't even know how this happened. I do. I lied there thinking to myself. All of this thinking, and I am still here on someone else's time. I mean I was 27 for Christ sake. How early can it really be to form a life of your own. It was my choice, and I was happy. Everyone left. A doctor came in, asked me a few questions, and then asked me to get back into the wheel chair.

"I think it is time for me to leave", I say to him.

"That's not possible mam, you practically killed your brother in-law. We have to keep you here for some more inspecting."

"The house is made of wood, so I was 'practically' giving him back to trees. It could not have been that hard. I was not trying to kill him, I just wanted my wine."

I couldn't take any more of his speculation, so I get up to walk out. He stops me right at the door.

"Mam, I can't allow you to leave, not like this. Please, let us help you."

"What is this some intervention? I'm not under arrest am I ?"

He opens the door and Vincent is standing there in tears.

"You're happy too right? This is a new beginning for the both of us. We are going to live happily with our new edition to the family."

"Jah, you can't leave", he says.

"What, so you're my doctor too huh? Don't flatter yourself."

"Jah, you might lose your license."

"You don't know what I have been through. I have seen things on the job just as you have seen. I have sleepless nights, just as you."

"And that Jah is why you should stay, let them figure you out a little bit more"

"You caused this!", I yell out to him.

CAN YOU KEEP A SECRET?

" I wanted to go to sleep and all you told me was to go to bed. You didn't even come in and check on me. I had to sleep in our bed all night without you. My dreams were combining and flipping realms, and I was shaking in my sleep. Where were you? So, don't tell me what to do Vincent. You are not my husband, and I would be proud to raise our daughter without you." I take my ring off and hand it back to him.

"What?", he said.

Before he could get anything else out, the nurses quickly grabbed me and pinned me to the chair.

"Well you could of said please."

By this second go round, I'm half asleep. There's no telling where we were headed. I heard a bing and woke up to be on the 3rd floor.

"Okay mam, please stand."

I'm already here, so might as well follow orders. I step on the scale.

"It looks like you have gained a bit of weight, for your age."

"Excuse me but I am pregnant. You ever thought of that."

They pay no mind to my statement and lead me to my room.

"Why am I here", I ask again.

"We are still trying to figure that out mam, please have patience with us."

"Well, I'm already here, so do with me what you will. If you touch me, or destroy my child, you will not see the light of day again."

As I am walking to my room, I see people in a tv room to the right of me. I go lie down, and it's dark outside, so I don't even have the view of her to occupy my mind. I've never been in a mental institute before. The thought of it scares me shitless. I don't belong here with these mad people. I need to be at home, nurturing my daughter's visit. I look at the white walls and dull floor board and cry. I walk over to turn the lights off. I want it completely dark in here, so If I must call out to her, she has more than enough space to come to me. I'm crying uncontrollably now. I've lost everything, and I didn't even get to say goodbye to my last life. The only thing keeping me alive now is the thought of my child I just created. One of the nurses knock on the door and enters without permission.

"Mam, you have had a long night. I think these and some water might ease your stay", she says.

"What are those?"

"Vitamins."

"Vitamins at night. C'mon now. I am not a doctor, but those things are too big to be vitamins. Plus I am with child, so don't confuse me. You think you doctors and others that are in the medical field can just tell me anything, and expect me to jump at your bucking call. I am not a product of my society or your test rat. Don't trick me mam, your job is on the line."

"Are you threatening me Mrs. Gilbert"

"Oh now you know how to address me, and please don't act like a threat brings any danger to you. You get to go home at the end of the night. I don't. This type of stuff isn't new to you."

"So you agree that there is something wrong with your mental."

"What's it to you?"

CAN YOU KEEP A SECRET?

" I know you don't want to believe it, but I am here to help the best way I know how to."

"The best thing for you to do right now is leave.", I say to her helplessly.

"No problem. I will leave as soon as you take your meds for tonight."

"I just got here. Haven't even been present for more than 24 hours and you're telling me that the doctor has already prescribe something for me to take. Get out of here, mam."

"This is just to help you rest, so your mind is clear the next day and we can run some test to see the real issue to why you are with us. Your husband tells us that you haven't been sleeping for the last couple of days. You've been getting up throughout most nights roaming the house mumbling words that he can't comprehend."

"I've seen demons matched with spirits trying to break it's way through my shadows. Carving trees with my mind in the near fire pit, wishing I was on fire because I am out of place, out of mind, out of body. I am supernatural and this isn't my world. I belong somewhere else feeding the children and making motives clear as to why us adults are here. We're here to help. I have a calling, and my first task is to showcase it with love."

"I'm sorry you are going through this, I really am. Women like you come in everyday lost and seem upset about something we can't pick up on. I really am here to help you."

"I am not taking those 'vitamins'. Nothing you can say or do will make me take them. I am pregnant, and I want my journey to be as natural as possible."

"But if you're not well, do you really think you can give birth to a healthy baby?"

"Why can't you all take my case seriously. If I am telling you I am pregnant, then why are you giving me pills that could possible defect my unborn child's life. Now you tell me, is that healthy? No offense to you because I understand this is your job. However, if someone must talk to me during this time, can I please get someone with profound knowledge on my type of situation to prescribe me with what you are calling 'sleeping pills' that will not hurt my child. I will go crazy trying to protect her. I've never had kids before and I am not sacrificing her for myself. It would well enough be the other way around. Tell me you don't have any empathy for my child. All you guys have been doing all night is shoving me here and there, bossing me around. Yet none of you have not even acknowledged my presence much less what is growing in my stomach. If I'm not healthy, and I might not be according to your statistics and prefaced facts, then why won't you all help me and my little one. I'm not just going to hand her over to the system. I am an educated woman with a law degree, and I deserve some respect."

"How do you know your child is a girl?"

" A mother knows. Can you please escort yourself out of this room? I could really use some sleep", I reply.

"Alright Mrs. Gilbert, I will bother you no more. Have a goodnight."

I close my eyes. It's not like I can fall asleep, but I wasn't going to take those medications under any circumstances I repeat to myself. I ty and count sheep.

There's fog every where and people are passing around cups like it's the theme. I hear the music thumping in the background. I sit on one of the couches. Vincent is no where to be found. I could really use my husband right now. I don't know where I am. The smoke fills my chest, and I run to the bathroom for some air. Young women in high heels and short skirts are just flowing by. I wait in the stall until some of them clear out. I walk out. I'm barefooted and the floor is icy cold. I walk up to the mirror and look inside. I don't recognize this face at all. I blink once or twice and the face turns into a gremlin looking women. I step back. I slowly take another look. It's the same woman. Is that me?

"No child this is your mind's eye. This is how old you appear to be. You are stuck in the wrong body and that is not your child you are carrying", the figure said.

The smoke from the club is clogging the bathroom. I cough harder and harder. I see something in the fog. Oh God please let me be alive. The object walks closer towards me. It's her, the gremlin and she blow a puff of smoke in my face.

I wake up coughing uncontrollably. My body is cold, and I am dripping with sweat. This is going to be a long night. I get on my knees to pray. I want nothing more than to keep what is inside me, but if I must let go than I would like to go with it. I fell in love with someone I don't even know, and she is the only thing that is keeping me alive right now. She is the only reason I want to live. Am I that desperate God? Is it really depression that is attacking my mind? I get up and try to lie back down. I think of a place that brings me bliss. I think of the time I went parasailing with my dad back when I was a jit, or the time I would always travel for my job. Being up in the air, I connect to something much bigger than me. All my life I felt I was soul searching, and never found anything. I decided to stop searching, but I never gave up on the hope of renewing myself every so often. I wanted to let my soul confirms its existence naturally. Awhile I was searching, I felt I was forcing beauty upon myself. I took a mirror with me everywhere I went, and had a makeup bag while on trips. Why was I so consumed with perfection? Every curl must lay a certain way, and every feeling must resemble the way I walk. I'm tossing and turning trying to find comfortability in this cot of a bed. Well let me back track. It does have a head board and side boards, but the bed is crunchy. I don't know if there is plastic inside of it or not, but it is not soft. The sheets were the only thing that I could bare. They were thick and had the smell of the hospital. I'm grateful that I am here I guess. It gives me some time to rest and gather my thoughts. I wish I had my journal though. All off these thoughts and no where to disperse them. I feel out of order as if nothing works anymore. I turn over one last time to reach a comfort spot. Then I hear a bell, and over the intercom someone is calling for all patients to go out to the tv room and receive breakfast. I ignore the call and try to sleep some more. I hear someone knock at my door,

"Excuse me Mrs. Gilbert, but your breakfast is here."

"No thank you", I reply.

Having your belly full, might allow you to get some rest. I think you should come out. Maybe chatting with the others will make your stay more comfortable."

I get up, and sit on my bed with my eyes half shut.

"How do you know I didn't sleep last night?"

"We have cameras in all of the rooms, so we saw your irritability. Plus, you were mumbling slight things in your sleep. That shows us you didn't really rest last night. Do you want to talk about what you were going through, or what might have been going through your head. That will give us a better understanding of what to prescribe you with."

"I'd rather just attend breakfast."

CAN YOU KEEP A SECRET?

I grab my long blanket they provided me with and walk out unto the hallway. They keep it so cold in here. How could anyone sleep?

I wait in line for my breakfast plate. I grab my plate once my name is called and find a chair out in the mixing area. There is another room beside the tv room, except it doesn't have a tv in there. I just look around. There is nothing colorful about this place. No pictures of relatives, no paintings or drawings. Blank walls is all that surrounds this place. If they really want to make someone feel comfortable they would spruce up the colors a bit. It's like I am preparing for death in here. I lift the lid on my plate. Pale scrambled eggs, one sausage link, fruit and a cup of milk is all that is on my plate. Oh, and a menu for what we would like for lunch. Great, a choice of our own. Finally. Someone offers me the remote, and I tell them I don't watch much tv.

"No thank you."

"I can tell you don't want to be here. Then again, who would want to be in this place. Here, I'll tell you the secret to getting out of here. You must sleep or at least look like you are sleeping. They say a full night's rest keeps the mind flowing smoothly at night to prepare you for the next day. Therefore, if you don't sleep, you are not prepared to start your day", this guy tells me.

"Well thanks for the insight, but that's the only way out of here? There's no escape method that you have?"

"Ahaa good luck. They have cameras and body guards blocking the door at all times, especially at night", he tells me.

"What's a woman like you doing here anyway. You seem fine to me."

"The eye is truly appealing sir, and I am pregnant for the matter."

"Pregnant or not, there's more to your story."

"What makes you think I would like to share?"

"Listen mam, I am just here to pass the time. I want to be no burden to you or your situation."

"They don't know what is wrong with me, or at least they won't spill the beans. I had a mental breakdown, so I am here with you to get what they may call is 'help'."

"Do you want help? Cause it seems to me you have it all figured out."

CAN YOU KEEP A SECRET?

"Thank you for asking. I'm not sure if 'want' is the word I am looking for to describe what I 'need'."

"Well no one wants to take pills all of the time."

"Okay Mrs. Gilbert, your next. Please sit in this chair, and uncross your legs for me, so we can check you blood pressure. No need to be afraid mam, we are just making sure everything is squared away with you", a nurse asks.

I do as she ask. As I am sitting in the chair, I admire the man in front of me. He has soft eyes like my husband, but he is tall and skinny. He could almost go for an NBA basketball player. He catches me staring at him, so I quickly look away. I look back to see if he is looking, and for certain he is. I can't help but drift. I want to be everywhere he is, and I would love to know more about him or at least why he is here. I throw him a smile and turn my head. My turn is over, they tell me everything is fine, but I don't stay to hear the rest. My mind is tired from being up all night, so I go lie back to my room. I don't think I barely even touched my plate. I should have eaten, for the baby's sake. I go back to see if it's still there. It is, but they are taking it away. I stop and ask if I cold just have the milk. They give it to me without question, so I thank them kindly. As I am heading back to my room, soft eyes stop me and asks for my name.

"Mrs. Gilbert", I say to him.

"I don't want to know you formally mam, and I promise to respect your boundaries on a account of your marriage. I will only take this as far as you'll let me. Can I have your first name."

"Jahanna."

"Can I call you Jah perhaps?"

"That's what everyone calls me, so I guess it won't be a bother for you to. Now can I have your name."

"Christopher. I don't really have a nickname. People call me Chris, but in my defense it's a bit demeaning because my mother never called me that. She worked hard to raise me. The least I can do is respect the name she has given me."

"Your mother must have been beautiful. I can tell by your eyes. You have really captured her feature nicely."

"Is that why you couldn't keep your eyes off me in there?"

"Precisely. You remind me so much of my.. Well I like you okay. You are the only nice looking thing that it is even in here."

"I was thinking the same. They really don't make this place home. As if it is supposed to be I know, but still."

"Yes, I know. Christopher take this for no more than what it really is, but I am very tired and would like to lie down."

"You didn't get much sleep either huh."

"I guess we are both stuck with each other for a while."

"Could I keep you company?"

"I glance at him with a smile. I don't think that's possible even if I wanted you to. This is not a hotel", I say to him.

"Can I..."

"Good bye Christopher", I say to him as I close my room door behind me."

What a man, I think to myself. I have a man, I remind myself also. He is nice to look at though. Let me get off the subject of him though. It is way to early to be thinking of someone in that way. It must be the collagen. There's two beds in my room now. Oh no, I hope I don't get a roommate. I can't handle someone else's thoughts right now, and I for sure don't want to converse with anyone. I lie on the one closest to the window. The sun is almost up. I lie on my back and rub my belly. One rub at a time, and I can feel my stomach growth

CAN YOU KEEP A SECRET?

within the movement of the sun. It slowly rises, and I slowly rub in oval motions. What bliss it is to grow with the sun's melanin. Someone knocks at the door. Even though I am not, I yell out that I am naked. The nurse said she will wait until I got dressed. Well she's going to be waiting for a while because I do not feel like getting up, moving about, or looking at her face. I'm tired. I try to close my eyes for a little bit, and the knocking continues. I listen to every thump and rub my belly to the sound of it. Very slow and controlled just like the pounds from the door. It stops, and I hear footsteps as if she is walking away. Finally, now I can have peace. I knew she would come back, so I decided to have a little more me time. Their not going to let me get any sleep anyway. Might as well have fun with them a little bit. I got up, and all of a sudden I felt my stomach drop. Wow, imagine what rubbing can do in just the matter of seconds. She's growing. Of course, not noticeably, but she is growing. I wanted to connect with myself more, and now I am feeling every little change of her inside me. Not a moment that I miss, because I am fully alert and aware of where she is. I lean back to better my posture. It makes a difference, but I swear it feels like I am seventy years old having a full gown baby inside.

CAN YOU KEEP A SECRET?

I have my own bathroom inside my small yet spacious room. I walk inside. I notice someone quite simple, yet with no beauty. It feels angelic to look at her. A face without makeup just pure insanity, how can someone have such soft features. A force takes over me, and I punch the mirror nearly breaking my knuckles. I feel no pain, but there is blood and glass sliding down my hands. A loud thump, and no one knows where it came from. I walk outside with blood dripping everywhere. A nurse rushes over to me.

"Oh my gosh what happen? Can you explain this?", she asks.

"I think I deserve my own room", I reply.

"Well we'll have to see, but first I mean can we at least get you cleaned up?"

"I suppose."

A nurse takes me to my room and sits me down.

"Mam what's going on. You're the only patient that we seem to know nothing about. You don't come out your room for no one, and you act out so courageously. What happened before you got here", a male nurse says to me.

CAN YOU KEEP A SECRET?

He's dark skin, almost jet-black dark, and his eyes... He has like a mini fro mix with a fade going on top of his head. I can tell he is young, but not that young. He looks nothing like my husband, and much taller as a matter of fact.

"I had sex", I reply.

"Okay and? Everybody does that?"

"Not the way that I had sex. I became someone I couldn't recognize. I lost myself on his chest. It's like I fell asleep, or died one. I had angels coming in and out my ear, telling me what to do and where to place my fingers. It was like I was mapping out something in that very room. Though I was happy afterwards and seemed complete. My body was shattering on the inside, and then I smiled because I felt something arise in me. Now I'm here. What do you make of that?"

He looks at me in confusion.

"So you are here because you had crazy sex?"

"We made love sir. Just because it is not something that you are not used to does not conclude crazy."

"I'm sorry. Your story is so bazaar. I can't wrap my head around it much."

"So don't, just help me."

"How?"

"I got to get out of here. This place is only holding me back."

"You and I both know that is not going to happen. Even if I wanted to."

"Do you want to?"

"Um..I think this conversation is going left and a bit inappropriate."

"Listen, I just had a full-blown conversation with you with clear feedback, and looked in your eyes sincerely. Now you tell me is there really anything wrong with me or am I just playing stupid?"

He gets up and walks out, and then remembers that my hand is still bleeding. He has no choice but to come back. He does, and he cares for my cuts without any words. Though he looks into my eyes as if he knows something that I don't.

"Please", I say to him.

He shakes his head. "I'm only here to do my job Mrs. Gilbert, not to help you escape some lost cause. You need to be here."

CAN YOU KEEP A SECRET?

He finishes wrapping my hand up , tells me I'll have surgery later if I need it, and exists my room. I cry at the sound of his footsteps, and then I remember who I am. I am a queen, and I shed for no one. If they want to keep me here, then I will stay here, forever.

Chapter 9

"Time for lunch. All patients, please report to the main room for your meal", I heard over the intercom. I'm still running on no sleep, and they constantly want to stuff food into my mouth. I'll be fat as a cow by the time I lay my head down. I only leave my room to see Christopher. I look like a zombie however, and I'm dragging my feet. I get my tray and go into the room. I see Christopher sitting at one end of the table, so I sit in the opposite direction of him. I just want him in my view. I look at my food, and it looks tasteless. No salt, no seasoning, this is going to be fun to eat. I look at Christopher, and I see him eating his meal so dreamlessly. How can he enjoy this treatment? Ooh he just stuck out his longue and wrapped it around his fork. Damn, I know he can feel my pressure. He doesn't look my way not once. Maybe he's trying to play the game, and make our connection unknown. I look down at my food again. I make designs in it with my fork. A dragon here, a hog there. The spaghetti looks like hair and it's making my stomach turn. Oh yeah, I'm pregnant. I must eat to feed her. I look across the table to see everyone tearing into their food. I mean it's not that great. I wish I had a cheese burger. Hospital café food is always the best. They'll never treat us to some up here though. I try to eat, and then I feel pressure from someone else. Someone's looking at me. I dive into some spaghetti and look up. With a fork in my mouth, I see that is Christopher who is waving at me with his eyes. Don't make me blush boy. He reaches for his ice cream. The way he opened it, lick the top flap just makes me quiver inside. He takes his spoon and rest the ice cream on his tongue. I look away before I catch of glimpse of others watching. This is too much for tv. I kind of like it though. This is the best excitement that I have gotten all day. I quickly finish my food and get up from the table. I couldn't bare any more. He does the same. As I walk over to put the tray back on the cart, I look over to him and ended up dropping my entire tray on the ground. Damn it, these hormones have me jumping all over the place. Why is one guy turning my life around? He stares at me as he helps me clean it up.

"Thank you", I say kindly.

"No problem Jah", he repeats back.

CAN YOU KEEP A SECRET?

Man how does he know my name. I don't remember giving him that much info, yet he said it so comfortably as if he has known me all these years. I smile and place my tray back up on the cart. I walk back to my room. Soon after, the nurse comes in.

"Hi Mrs. Gilbert, I am Luanne. I will be taking care of you today. Before we start, how are you feeling today."

"Oh mam, please. No disrespect, however I am in a mental institution with locked windows and blank walls to keep me company. How do you think I feel. No matter of answering that, can you skip to why you are visiting me?"

"Well, Mrs. Gilbert, asking you how you are feeling each day is part of us helping you get better or too feeling up to par. I'm just trying to give you the proper treatment, so that you can go home and see your family. I hear that you haven't been sleeping?"

"How can I? You guys are always coming into my room throughout the day checking in on me, while I am trying to rest. Even when it is time for bed, you guys still come bothering me in the middle of the night to do some more checking in on me. What sense does it make to check on me while I am sleep? I am asleep, so what more validation do you guys really need", I say to her sounding clear and irritated.

"Actually mam, our records show that you have not been getting any sleep at all. It says here that you were tossing and turning all night and that you even got out of bed a few times."

"Your point", I reply.

"Okay. I see you are not going to make this easy for me. Let's skip to the main part to why I visited you today. It says here on your chart that you believe you are pregnant?"

"Yes."

"Mam, your urine sample came back hours ago. Has not anyone given you any update?"

"Isn't that why you are here?"

"Your test came back negative. Mrs. Gilbert, you are not pregnant."

"How absurd can you really be? I know what is growing inside of me regardless of what your test says."

"Mrs. Gilbert we cannot treat you to any vitamins or medication regarding a pregnancy that you don't have. We have to treat you as a regular patient with proper medication going towards your diagnosis. Also, we keep people here longer under false allegations"

"And what am I diagnosed with?"

"It's hard to say, because it is still early, and the doctor has to see you a few more times. Right now you are being treated with schizophrenia. You must cooperate with us Mrs. Gilbert, so we can find out a little more about what is going through your mind at night and during the day. That is the reason for our frequent visits", she says to me.

"Are you done?"

"Will you take your meds for me?"

"No."

"Then you will have to stay a while longer. You don't take your meds, then you won't get any sleep."

"I don't even know what I am taking. You guys are just shoving things into my face without any empathy for my situation."

"And what is your situation Mrs. Gilbert?"

"I am pregnant and that is that. Man created your machine, so there is likely to be errors within it. How do you know I am not just a special case, and your machines cannot pick up on my fluids. I will stay here if it takes for you guys to see my point. Maybe I'll just stay for nine months. Is that okay with you Nurse Luanne? Or how about this allegation…If I believe in God and you don't, would you still keep me here?"

"The doctor will see you soon Mrs. Gilbert, please try to get some rest", she says as she gets up and walks out of the door.

How dare they disregard my pregnancy. It's a setup, it must be. Someone is pulling the strings tight on this one.

I'm tired, and there is just no point in me attempting to rest. My mind just rambles anytime my head touches the pillow. I know I need medication. I'm not against that, but I am a mother first. I can't do it without her. I just can't. I get up and decide to exercise my legs a little bit. I walk out of my room and into the hallway. I see Christopher down the hall going into his room. There is another office to the left of me filled with nurses and techs. I see this old lady sitting in a chair next to one of the computers. Her chair is bigger than the rest, so my guess is that she is over the rest. The glass pane doesn't allow me to see her straight on. I see her sitting in her chair, but it is like the glass is shadowing a part of her, and I can only see her at an angle. There is this plug looking wire in the shadow behind her. Maybe that is for me, and maybe I am the only one that can see it. I look to left and right of me, and no one is around. No one behind the glass is paying attention to me either. I try to connect the plug of the computer to an outlet without making notice to anyone else. Is this part of my mission? I stare harder at it, thinking that maybe the old lady is the outlet. She seems weary and dried out, as if she yearns for inspiration. Wiping her eyes, yawning, I try to focus on her movements. I don't see any flashing lights, but all of a sudden, the shadow is gone and her computer is in my preview. I have successfully connected. I turn to walk down the hallway towards Christopher's room without any one noticing. I have reached the end, and the window is in front of me. I sit down and crisscross my legs. Something is coming to my mind, a song perhaps. I try and sing the words, "the way you making me feel." Except it isn't coming out right and I don't remember the next line. I try harder. I close my eyes and envision the words. My tongue gravitates towards these vibration and I let out a loud cry. I was hoping that Christopher would come out and join in song with me, but I think that maybe he is sleep. I don't feel their footsteps, but nurses start to surround me and pick me up by my forearms and carry me back down the hallway. I'm singing tunes with my eyes closed all the way there. I open them and I see I am back in my room. The door shuts. I walk over to the second bed closest to the window.

"Alright Mike, now what. What do you want me to do?", I say to the bed. I picture him lying there with me rising my hands over the bed. I keep the tune going since to me, I have never sung before a day in my life. I don't remember all of the words, which is so bazar to me. I start to create my own. "You don't know what you have done to me, a see is a saw but it is an eye for me. How do I picture time without a life to see? They tear you down but it is all a lie to me."

"Don't stop" is what I hear in the back of my head. I keep going with "this is the way you making me feel. Tell me twice and I'll.."

"It's yours J", I hear again.

I then adjust my feet quickly and spin around to the door. I must walk out. It is now my time to leave. I cannot stay here any longer. I must break free. I open the door and walk back up to the office. It is now 7oclock at night.

"I must go now", I say to the old lady.

"Wait until the shift changes", she replies.

I turn my head to the side than quickly back at her.

"You don't understand, someone is waiting for me outside of this thing"

"We'll see you when the shift changes", she says again.

I hear laughter in the background.

"YOU GAVE HIM TO ME, NOW I MUST GO!", I shout back at her.

She said nothing.

"DO YOU KNOW WHO I AM, I AM A LEGEND! I DON'T BELONG HERE AND I CANNOT STAY UNDER ANY CIRCUMSTANCES. OPEN THE ELEVATOR!"

She still said nothing. I gather my thoughts. What a way to get someone to do something for you than to be nice to them. I try and change my voice and proceed with my request.

"Please let me out of here. This isn't my home", I try and say calmly yet stern.

"When the shift changes", she says again.

CAN YOU KEEP A SECRET?

I had enough. I walk over to the elevator and stand there in front of this six foot tall lady.

"I have to go. Please let me out", I say to her.

"I cannot let you do that, and you cannot leave Mrs. Gilbert"

"That is not my name!", I say as I try to push her to the elevator to maneuver my way through. I hear the elevator ding and someone comes out. I push my way through the body guard and make my way into the elevator. I'm in. All of these buttons are long foreign to me though, and before I can get a jist of what they mean, all of the nurses come in the elevator swarming me. I fight my way to the buttons and try to press the number one. Shit, there's a slot for a key to go there. I keep pressing, but nothing happens and they soon carry me out of there. I almost had it. I almost went home. Tears flow down my eyes as I am being carried back to my room.

"Alright Mrs. Gilbert that is enough out of you, now stay here until it is time for dinner", the bodyguard says to me. I sit on my bed with anger and disappointment rolling around in my thoughts. I was almost home, I said to myself. No one wants to let me go. I try and sing since all I have left to myself is this crusty ol' bed and my beautiful voice that I have now discovered. I hold my stomach in my arms and rock it to the sound of my voice.

Hi dear. It's me. Would you gather up this picture, of me. It's my duty to protect thee. Trust me, no one is coming in between you or me. Can you believe we're in this place together; having trials and tribulations because I've conceive a new era. They tell me they cannot find you up on the screen, but trust me no one's false belief will hold you against me. Yet I'm not sure what I'll do next, or where I will go. I didn't mean to stir up this pot, but I will have guaranteed to rock this boat. If only your father was here to see how beautiful you are. You're so young, but I can feel you in my sleep. I get nauseated from being in this cold room all of the time. I will, however, keep you safe and out of harms way. The doctor is coming soon, but I already know what he is going to say. Oh dear, if only you knew how much you mean to me. I will try to explain it all through this song entitled beautifully. This is not the end, so don't fret for me. I just need you to stay, stay with me, and write this note for me. I can see that you are one of a kind, and a dream to be. My dear this is the beginning of a natural prophesy.

I have fallen asleep, and it feels so great for it to happen in symphony. I drift off. This time my dream is coming in double. We are back at the waters with my belly well rounded. I slide into the water and let my face go under. I swim as far as I can until I am in the middle of the river. I turn on my back and let the water lift me up. Only my belly is what you can see from afar. Letting the wind hit my body with such passion. I hear nothing else around me except the birds chirping in the trees, and the trees waving in the wind. I feel the lily pads and the leaves touching me ever so gently. I close my eyes and let out my arms. It feels like summertime alright, but I don't mind the tan. I let my body fall under the water, and I swim some more. I go as far as I can until I have to tread between the waters to breathe. I think to myself, looking far out, that what if I just ended it right here, right now. If I could just sacrifice our lives, and it will all be over and the nonsense will stop. I can't hold myself up any longer. The ripples are hitting my face hard. I can't face the waters no more. If I go under at this moment in time, then at least I will be dying within earth's crevasses. I gasp for air and look out one last time. So beautifully, yet so treacherous out there. That life isn't for me. This is my life now, goodbye.

I wake up gasping for air. I see the nurses surrounding me. Woah, did they feel that too? I'm shaking tremendously and I ask them,

"What do you guys want. I'm not happy and I have fallen into a deep depression being here. Please don't take anything else from me."

I lie back down with tears creeping down my face.

"We came in here because you wouldn't answer our knocks. We decided to come in anyway. We saw that you were sleeping, but the strangest thing happened. You weren't breathing and we couldn't check for a pulse. We were in the process of taking you to the emergency room, but you woke that very next second. How are you feeling? Well let me tell you this. You have a visitor, and it seems urgent that he sees you at once. I think it is your husband, Mrs. Gilbert", nurse Luanne says to me.

CAN YOU KEEP A SECRET?

"I don't want to see anybody Luanne."

"Mam it's your husband, and he's worrying himself sick about you. Do you not care?"

I look at her in disgust and turn my head back towards the window.

"Can you guys give me a minute with her please. I think I can be of assistance", an unfamiliar voice says to the others.

"Hi Mrs. Gilbert, I am John Whittaker, your doctor for today. What was it that made you come up for air so drastically. I mean this in the lightest way possible, but did you have a nightmare?"

"It wasn't exactly a nightmare. I was more in a relaxed state of mind. I was where I needed to be. I was home."

"What happened there, if you don't mind me asking?"

"Everything made sense there. I didn't have to think or try to be something that I am not like I am here. I was free of bondage."

"It sounds like you got some sleep with being so relaxed. Your heart rate stopped though, so maybe you were too relaxed. I don't see how though because you haven't taken any medications that could have or may have altered your transitioning. Well they did tell me you were a special one. Let me get this straight. You have refused any type of medical treatment, why?"

"Your guys don't know what is wrong with me, so I don't see the need to put something into my system that may or may not be what I need. I can't trust your system or your method off choice. I'm fine with taking medication to solve what it is that is altering my thoughts. But.."

"Stop! There! Sorry, I do not mean to scare you, but you have just reached a break through. Okay, now we are getting somewhere. You say that you are having altered thoughts? Describe those thoughts for me."

"You're lucky you got that out of me. I haven't been talking to anyone much. Everyone just seems to just push pills in my face begging for me to take them. I don' t know about these thoughts that in my head. They are very aggressive and interchangeable. One minute I think you are saying this and the next minute I'm confused."

"Would you say that you are depressed?"

"Being in here makes me think I am. There's no one around me that can understand what I am saying. Everybody thinks I am jamming my words together or giving false accusations."

"What false beliefs do they perceive?"

"They're keep telling me that I am not pregnant, but I know I am."

"How do you know you are? Have you taken any test or had a urine sample ran for testing?"

I lied and said, "I took one before I came here."

"Well this is the first I am hearing of this. I'm sorry, but the nurses have stated that they are getting their readings from the urine sample you gave. Now before you say anything, I was not trying to trick you when I asked you that question. My prior knowledge is a blank slate the minute I talk to my patients. I try to hear out both sides of the story before I make any kind of judgement", he said.

"So you believe me right? I'm telling the truth?"

"Now I can't make judgement from your reasonings just yet, but I will give you my word that I will look more into it. Let me ask you a couple more questions though, so we can get you your proper meds. Why haven't you been talking to anyone here?"

"I don't know anyone, and not that interested to get to know anyone. I like Christopher though. He's nice to me. I wish more people were as gentle as you and him are. My husband showed up today, but I did not care for his visit."

"He's the only person you know Mrs. Gilbert. What made you reject his request?"

"I don't really know. I have no words to describe what I was feeling. I just couldn't bare to look at him anymore."

"But when you go home, you will be going home to him correct?"

"I suppose."

"I'm not understanding. Can you elaborate your thoughts for me?"

"That's the thing. I don't know what I am thinking. Half of the time, I do not know why I don't want him or anyone for that matter to visit me. I know I love him even though I am not sure why. I don't really want to talk anymore. Can I leave this room?'

"Sure Mrs. Gilbert", he says.

"Please call me Jah."

"Okay. Well Jah, you have given me more than enough information to consider your performance. I will get back with you soon. Thank you for wanting to talk to me today. I really appreciate it."

"Thank you for wanting to listen Dr. Whittaker."

Well now that is over, I can finally go talk to my lover. I see him immediately as I open the door.

"Hey Chris", I say to him.

He smiles and keeps walking. I follow him. Everywhere he goes I'll follow. I think he is catching on to what I am doing. He stops and turns around.

"Why are you following me?"

"Well I love you of course."

"You barely even know me madam. I could be bad for you."

"I know you enough to know that you are not bad at all."

"And how do you figure that? What, Did you take a glimpse at my chart or something?"

"No, but you just told on yourself."

"Love at first sight huh? Aren't you married Jah?"

"I'm not. I don't love him."

"Who's playing tricks now. It's either you are married and you don't love him, or you aren't married at all."

"It's both Christopher. There is no games between you and I."

"Do you have a home Jah?"

"I don't."

"Why don't you come run away with me after it is all said and done. I'm a basketball player and I can really treat you to a life you have never seen before. I know you are a lawyer and can take care of yourself, but I want you to come with me. Say you will go, when I give you my mark?"

"Sure Christopher. It's whatever you say."

I love his smile, even if he has a gap in the middle of his teeth. He heads back to his room and I follow him once again. The nurses caught on to my mischief and stopped me before I got any closer to him. I saw the inside of his room. It seemed much bigger than mine. Maybe a room for two, it was supposed to be. As the nurses point to my room, I glance over at the next room and can see a woman shouting at a wall. To my right, an older man seemed to be cutting himself. I thought this was the perfect distraction. I yell for the nurses to come take a look. Three of them rushed out immediately, and I thought this was just perfect. I quickly make a slight turn and head to Christopher's room. I look behind me, but I see no one. I open the door. Trying to stay hidden from the room camera, I hide in the bathroom and whisper Christopher's name.

"Jah is that you?"

"Sshh, the camera can pick up sound." I say as he tries to peak around the corner.

"Act natural and make your way to the bathroom. Don't come to quick but come now."

He sits down for a minute acting as if he is pondering on some thoughts. He gets up and holds onto his stomach as if he is sick and in need of throwing up. Here's here.

"Kiss me", I say to him

"I don't think we can get away with this."

"Well if you won't then I will." I go in for a kiss and he doesn't resist. Seconds go by and his tongue makes his way into my mouth. I pull back.

"Do me", I say calmly to him.

"What? We don't have enough time"

I drop my pants and say, "You're wasting time, now get to it."

I can tell he likes me dominance. He gives me compliments as he makes his way in. Ugh, wow, I haven't felt this in a long time. So good. He places one hand around my neck in an upright position. It was getting too much to bare. My nipples were hard, and my vagina was overflowing. I couldn't help myself, we had to stop. I push away and pull my pants up.

"I have to go", I say to him.

"You don't have to. You can stay if you like."

"That's the vagina talking. You know good well I cannot stay. This is not our home."

"It can be, or I can take you to mine", he says as I make my way out of the door, hoping the hallway camera's won't catch the sudden movement. I crawl the rest of the way. I reach my hand to open up my room door and close it back slowly. I made it. I am back in my room without any sudden peep. I lie down on one of the beds and look out the window. I can imagine what life is like out there. Everybody is so busy occupying intangible things that they can't even stop to think about what life would be like without those "things". I mean I am living proof of that statement, and my senses have incredibly heightened. It is not until we are chained away somewhere that we realize the importance of self and what it means to be aware of how the self-changes. I'm talking as if I know it all. I am the reason I brought myself in here. I know that now. There is no need to blame someone else, even thought that does make me feel better. I'm still on the search for my soul's purpose for even forming in this human body. It's like I have found myself all over again being in this room, or was it the penis that has me wanting to straitened up. They say you must want help to receive proper help. Well I would like for my help to come to me with an elevator key that leads to the first floor. I turn on my side away from the window. I'm seeing this glare on the wall. I'm not sure if it is there or my mind playing tricks on me again. I blink. It's still there. Now it is moving with my eyes. I think first that maybe it is the sun's reflection from staring outside too long, but I was not staring directly or near the sun to begin with. I blink again, and now it has split into two. I wonder what this could be much less of what it means. A nurse come in. I didn't even hear a knock. Now the figure appears to be on her face, as I position my eyes to get a clear view of her. Her face is changing shape and turning from pale to red. Her eyes are blood shot red. Woah, am I seeing this correctly or is the baby drawing pictures with my eyes. It is none of my doing.

"Hi Mrs. Gilbert, I am nurse Patricia and I will be taking care of you this evening. How are you feeling today?"

"Please don't come any closer. I do not know who you are, but your aurora is flashing red signals at me."

"I'm sorry I don't understand", she says as she takes a step further.

"DON'T, PLEASE!", I shout. I grab my chest feeling some type of pain coming from within. "YOU'RE HURTING ME."

"Mam, I am here to give you your meds the doctor has prescribe for you."

"GIVE HER BACK TO ME! YOU JUST CAN'T WALK IN HERE AND TAKE HER FROM ME", I cry.

"Your mother is also here to see you Mrs. Gilbert. Would you like for me to call her back?"

"LEAVE", I shout again.

"Okay, I'll go get her."

My mother walks in with a remorseful look on her face.

"Jahanna what is going on dear?"

I look the other way without saying a word.

"They say you are in some form of depressed state and that you believe you are pregnant. I want to believe you, but their test is speaking otherwise. What's going on with you?"

I look up and see Christopher walk by, thinking that I must continue out with the plan.

"You are not my mother", I say to her.

"Let me help you", she says as she grabs my hand to kiss it.

"OW", I cry out. "She's hurting me."

The nurses rush right over.

"You are not my mother, and I will not sit here and let you guys take anything away from me. Where is doctor Luanne? She believes in me. I WANT TO SEE DR. LUANNE."

"Mam, I'm going to have ask you to leave now."

"Are you kidding me? I barely got ten minutes with her. She is my daughter for Christ sake. Jahanna needs me. I don't like her being in here anymore than Jahanna does. She has completely changed personas these last couple of months. I don't care what it takes. Help her with this disease. She has not gotten any better since I last saw her. What are you guys doing in here just standing around pretending that she will be okay. I am her mother, and she does not even recognize me. Have kids one day and watch them grow up. Then find them in an uncontrolled environment withering away with depression in a hospital where there are more patients than doctors, and you tell me how you would feel watching it go down first hand. We don't pay you guys to sit and talk to her every day. There are medications out there for her. Find it! If something happens to my daughter under your guys supervision, you will not see the end of me. However, I will leave for now because she cannot bare my presence, and seems to be killing her inside. Hold her for as long as needed, but I will be back."

I start losing control over my mind. I begin yelling and tearing up things in my room. This does not seem to satisfy me, so I start banging on my window hoping that I can make a crack in it and see some light of day before the sun goes down, and I am stuck in this dark hole. The nurses grab me and pin me to the bed. I fight back and squirm for freedom. Then I get this prick in my side, and my eyes start to fall heavy.

Chapter 10

I am awakened with my husband sitting on the other side of my room. I get up and walk over to him. I lean in as if I am going to kiss him and draw back my right fist and punch the daylights out of him.

"I am sitting and drowning in these dark walls every day and night, while you get to parlay outside and what not", I say as I walk to the door with my back turn to him. LEAVE ME ALONE! I am tired of all of you visiting me thinking that you are helping when you are not. This treatment is something I must deal with on my own. I am in here because of YOU! You went and implemented your seed in me, and now the doctor's can't even find her! They think I am lying and delusional", I break to my knees and say. "DON'T TOUCH ME. You cannot help me. No one can, so do me the favor and leave." I walk out and go sit in the tv room to find Christopher watching a gory movie. I sit across from him. As Vincent is leaving the building, he catches me talking to Chris and walks in.

"It is you! You are the reason my wife does not love me anymore!"

He rushes over to Christopher and starts to take his anger out on him by hitting him in the face, stomach, chest repeatedly. Christopher tries to fight back, but he is on the ground now. I stand up to get out the way. A small smile comes across my face, as I am looking out unto this ridiculous fight. Then I remember it is me they are fighting over, so I walk quietly back to my room as the nurses push me out of the way to get Vincent off Christopher.

As they are carrying Vincent out of the hospital he yells back, "It's him! He's in there! That is your guy right there."

I laugh uncontrollably to the sound of his voice. I don't bother checking on Christopher. I know he'll be fine. I mean we are in a hospital.

The nurse comes in my room and slams the door.

"What in the hell are you doing Mrs. Gilbert!? You have caused such trouble in this hospital! Why?!"

"I didn't ask for this."

"Oh, please, enough playing victim, you know what you are doing!"

CAN YOU KEEP A SECRET?

"Do I? You guys surely know what you are doing or do you not because I have still yet to receive my proper medications. Therefore, nurse, you tell me. Do I really know what I am doing? I am a sick patient waiting to be treated."

"Jahanna, we have tried to give you your meds"

"Under what circumstances were those the correct ones. According to Dr. Whitaker, he is still invested in my case. I am not taking anything until I hear word from him. Oh and we are using first names now? What happen to Mrs. Gilbert?"

"I don't know what will happen to Mrs. Gilbert. If you keep disrupting the peace in here, your mind will be so far gone that they will have no choice but to arrest you."

"Is that a threat Luanne. I don't take well to those. I'll play your game and be silent, however I will do this my way."

"I don't think there's anything wrong with you in my opinion. You are just here to take up space. We don't need you."

"Yet you need my money, so you all have made the choice of keeping me here."

"Not for long. Oh and by the way you stink, please go shower", she says as she exist my room.

CAN YOU KEEP A SECRET?

She was right. I don't remember the last time that I showered. I get undress and go take a shower. Too bad they don't have robes. Then again, this is not supposed to be a luxury experience. I run the water for a little bit waiting on the toilet for the water to get hot. Christopher might be mad at me at this point. I am queen though, so I'm sure he'll understand. I touch the water with my hand. It feels nice. The only time I can unwind is in this moment right here. I step in. I run the rag over the water and squeeze it out all over my body. I look down and see my stomach getting bigger. I lather up with some soap and begin wiping myself down. I check the tone in my voice to see if I still have that harmonious voice. I do. I hum a little bit to warm up my vocal cord.

"There is this light at the end of the future. Oh how I wish I could see your mother. She happens to not be here in this moment. However, I will find and seek for her return. Who should I listen to? Where should I turn? Is this a mountain, or will I just burn? My thoughts become too deep for me to bare your sight. I wish that I could look deep inside your eyes. This is my time now to give you back to God. In hopes that you will return soon, so I can hold you. They say you are nothing but a hallucination. My feelings for you remain the same. Could I go with you to that secret place? I am not sure how much more I can take. Fighting for you is all I ever believed, but now you are shedding, shedding your fears from me. When it is time, I will come for you again. So, don't forget me, my dear child. I am only doing what I feel is right. Go and go as far as you can. Only return with the shape of God's hand. For you, I will do my best to live and prosper. I hope that you live somewhere in happiness happily ever after."

As I finish this symphony, I feel something warm oozing out of the lower part of my body. I look down to find myself dripping with blood in huge clumps. I've lost her. She's gone. I sit down in the shower, while the rest spill out. I count to ten to try and calm my nerves, but the tears keep flowing down the side of my face. I take my hand and rub it across the wall. That doesn't satisfy me any, so I take my knuckles and rub them against the wall. Harder and harder I begin to draw blood on the wall. I scrape against it a few more times, hoping that the pain will turn numb. I can't feel a thing. I shove my knuckles into the wall and that time I felt it. The pain that I've been searching for has finally arrived. Something that gives me a reason to live again. I see I have created a face on the wall. It looks like a newborn baby. No hair just yet, but very piercing eyes. I run my hand over and let out the words "I am sorry to have let you go so soon."

I get up to wash myself off. Now my finger is burning with pressure. I don't mind it though. It is a little something that reminds me of her. I wash off my face full of tears, and rinse down the rest of my body. I turn the water off and grab for my towel. Drying myself off, I feel even more worried than I did when I walk into the bathroom. I open the door. Without putting any clothes I go lie down.

The covers feel fresh against my body even though I am aware that they are not. It doesn't matter to me though. Nothing really can bring me pleasure at this point no matter how hard I try. I look outside to see the sun going down and I cry. It's something about these tears that are so addicting. I am incomplete now and have this whole in my chest that doesn't seem to want to go away. I close my eyes. Before I could even get into my dreams, I hear a knock at the door. It's Dr.

Whitaker. I tell him to give me a second, while I get myself together. I grab some clothes my mother left for me and put them on.

"Okay you can enter", I tell Dr. Whitaker.

I sit on my bed, while I listen to him talk.

"Okay, Mrs. Gilbert. You seem to be everyone's favorite patient today. How did feel after all of that took place?"

"I felt nothing. I didn't feel sad for Christopher, and I was not proud for my husband that he got all his anger out. I haven't been feeling much of anything lately. Just taking up space I suppose."

"No mam, never that. Do you think that there is any way that you might be depressed from loosing your child?"

"How do you know about that?'

"Well her death is all over the news. It seems to be that she died in an atrocious accident late last night. Could that be the reason you are still trying to hold on to her?"

"What do you mean car accident? I did not have any kids before the one I have claimed to have when I first walked in here."

"Well, she has your last name and your husband has identified her body."

"What did she look like?"

"I'm surprise you aren't aware of this. She has dreadlocks just as you, and she was beautiful to say the least. Why do you feel as if she doesn't belong to you?"

"I'd have to talk to Vincent about this more. Save me the details please. I have already lost someone close to me."

"You mean your daughter?"

"No, my unborn child. Listen I know what your stats say, but I know what I felt. I even got nauseas to the sight of pizza, and that is one of my favorite foods. It doesn't matter now. You guys are right, and I am wrong. I do not have an embryo within my stomach."

"This isn't a plea to decide who is right or wrong mam. We just didn't understand what you were going through. I understand that your symptoms matched perfectly to a standard pregnant woman. However nothing was showing up on our board. I do apologize for both of your loses. Is it safe to say that we can now treat you and give you some medication for depression?"

"Oh, sir I have more than that. I think I am more powerful than you can imagine."

"Do you mind if we perhaps run a CAT Scan on you. It could be beneficial for you. Maybe something in your brain is not connecting or has an off switch that we are not aware of."

"Do whatever you feel is right sir. I am a patient in this hospital, so I will comply."

"Thank you, Mrs. Gilbert. We will see if we can get your husband back up here, maybe to bring you comfort I hope."

"No thanks, I rather not. I'll just see him once I am home. Thank you for your time. Goodnight."

Before I can get any sleep, the usual comes to my door.

"Mam, we called for dinner. Do you mind coming out here and getting your tray? Before you answer, I'd like for you to know that it does help with taking your meds this late at night."

"Listen, you do not have to go into your information sheet and tell me all the goods of taking my medication. I know this already, and I am ready to take them. Before I take them though, I would like to see if I can get a printed out description of exactly what it is that you will be giving me.. I don't mind taking the medication, but I would like to read what I am putting into my body."

"Sure Mrs. Gilbert, of course. I will get that too you right away. Thanks for complying with us", she says.

"Yeah whatever."

I walk out into the hallway and into the tv room to find no sight of Christopher. I look around one more time and still no sight of him. I ask one of the techs serving the food where he might have gone, and she tells me that he is gone. She won't say where, but just those few words she said to me was enough to have me in despair. I can't believe he would leave so quickly without even saying goodbye.

"Where can I find him", I asked her.

"Mam we aren't allowed to disclose information to people that are not family."

"He's my husband!"

"No mam, your husband, Mr. Gilbert, has left hours ago. Christopher does not have a wife."

"I thought you weren't suppose to disclose information remember."

CAN YOU KEEP A SECRET?

I try and push my way through the door. Banging on it even harder looking for Christopher and hoping he sees me where ever he is. The nurses grab me and I kick and push on the door some more. I don't know what this will solve, but it is helping me with getting all of my anger out. I tug on the door harder, and they just round up more nurses. This time they have me by my arms and feet. I try to strangle loose, but I ended up just flipping over to my stomach. Wow, so much energy I have for people I don't understand and feelings I can't choose from, because they are so twisted in my head. I don't know what I am feeling, but I am feeling something. I look up at the ceiling, as they carry me back to my room and cry a silent cry out for Christopher. I am back where I have started. Another nurse that didn't tussle with me approaches me with my food tray.

I walk off without touching it and close the door behind me. I am so distraught. The one person that understood what I was going through is now gone. What am I going to do without him by my side talking me through this disfunction? I know I have family, but they can only visit for such limited time. They want me in here. No thank you. No one wants to run away with me and escape this world of confusion. Christopher was willing to. He was probably going to find a way for us to break out of here. He didn't care for me though, or he would have said goodbye. I was just another fluzy to him. On top of the rest, I just found out that I have a fifteen-year-old daughter who was driving under age and died in a car accident. I can't bare anything else. Bring on the meds, please. Make me forget. The nurse comes in with sheets of paper and tells me that they are still siding with schizophrenia, so they have prescribed me with Prozac for anxiety and Olanzapine to help with the hallucinations while I am sleeping. How do they know all of these things. I only talked to the doctor, and I never mentioned anxiety being something that is giving me trouble. Although, it is giving me trouble. I get so excited about the free juice you get at night as a snack, and then get upset at the fact that the tv is always off when I walk into the room. It also says it will make me fat and bloated all the time. Great. As I read up on schizophrenia, it said here that I have rapid mood swings, deepened depression mix with multiple personalities. Well that sounds about right. The nurse comes back in and ask am I ready to take my medicine. I told her why not and took the pills with some water she provided.

Thirty minutes later, I start to feel the medicine working, and I feel quite high off them as I am watching tv. The awards show is on. All of the loud clapping and anxious speeches make me feel as if I am right there with them. Well it is live, so I guess that substitutes my emotions. Everything turns hazy and dim. The bright lights aren't a big help either. I hear someone talking. When I look over I find this old lady talking her head off in my ear. I never said a word to her, yet she is having a full conversation with me right at this moment. Something in me tickles my spine and I start laughing and laughing harder. It's probably the medication, and I have not gotten quite used to it. My stomach starts turning flips inside of me. It puzzles me for a minute, and then I remember I didn't eat. Shit. I go over to the office and explain to one of the nurses that I am super hungry and would greatly appreciate if I had something to eat. She said to me that is beyond past dinner. Since I do have to eat with the medication to settle these cravings and I am being polite this evening, she tells me to wait there and she will go grab something for me. If I would of known that I can get my way by just being pleasant to talk to, then I would have done this a long time ago. I don't think I have tried this method yet, only with the doctor.

The food is amazing. It may well be these high-intensified, mood upbringing medications as I mention again, but the food is gone within seconds. I haven't been eating much while I have been staying here. I've just been so distraught and out of touch with life that I haven't really thought of much of anyone else. Wow, and to think of the way I have been treating my family.

I quickly give the lady my tray and thank her deeply. I think I was thanking her too much because she says that it may be the meds talking and that now I just need to rest. I go into my room and lie down. No tears seem to fall this go round, but I am still lonely. I shut my eyes and try to get some medicated sleep. A dream comes to me again.

I am sitting in my car with my guy friend Titan. He looks at me the way my husband does when he wants something. This time though I do not feel any urges or sexual desires. He reaches over to grab my hand and I tell him "rules". We are simply friends, and there needs to be no confusion between the two.

"Rules you say? So I cannot do anything, correct?"

I nod my head.

"Where are you taking me", I asked.

"The beach. You say you always like to be by the water."

"Right, but this late at night?"

"I figure you might see something that interest you at this time of night. Maybe something will inspire you to.."

"Inspire me to do what?"

He looks at me again and smiles. Lord knows I would like to know what is up his sleeve. He is deviant, this Titan. He stops the car by this corner store and asked if I would like something to drink.

"Sure", I reply.

"Okay, I will be right back Jah, don't go anywhere", he says with a wink.

He comes back with only one drink, and it is an alcoholic beverage. I know because it is short and inside of a paper bag. He closes the car door.

"This is for you Jah, happy birthday!"

"Rules."

"You can't even accept my gift?"

"That is not a gift Titan, rules, remember."

"I won't try anything Jah, honest. I just want you to loosen up a bit. You seem stressed."

I grab the beer and look at him with a side eye. I tell him if he tries anything that I will kill him without a trace. I think it startled him enough to stop trying me. I mean I haven't seen this guy in years. A new day comes around, and he tells me that I am tensed.

We have arrived.

We get out the car, but before I could take anymore steps he tells me to stand by the car.

"What do you want me to do now?"

"I want you to suck me up."

"Rules Titan, NO!"

"How mad are you Jah?"

"Mad enough to strike you Titan. How could you do this, I thought you were my friend?"

"I am. But you have been letting guys walk all over you Jah, just to leave you in the dust. I heard what happened between you and Chris back at the hospital. He just left you after it was all said and done. You have nothing left but your family. What are you going to do about it? Suck me up, NOW!"

I yell back, "RULES TITAN, I AM NOT THE SAME PERSON I WAS IN THERE!"

"Show me. Get mad!"

I got close to him enough to feel his breath on my top lip. I draw back my hand again, and he grabs it and turn it towards the car.

"GET MAD! LET OUT YOUR ANGER JAH. YOU MUST GET THIS DEVIL OUT OF YOU."

Something clicked inside of my head and I start hitting, punching, and kicking the car. I began shaking it until it was on its side. I picked it up and shook it as I was hammering it down to the ground. Each time I broke something. That wasn't satisfying enough, so I kicked it some more, and this time I am screaming from my lungs. Pounding the car one punt at a time, I could feel my outer body vibrating and humming through my joints. I grab a hold of Titan, scrunched up his skin, and tell him that if he ever in God's name, ever and I mean ever touch me again like that or disrespect my wellbeing that I will bite off his man parts and stuffed them into his ass hole.

"You really don't want to mess with me", I say to him.

Chapter 11

I woke up with my body in shock and weak as can be. I sit up on the bed to try and stand up. I stand beside the bed and count to ten to try and calm my body down. I felt that click again and I began tearing up the sheets, ripping them up, and throwing them against the wall. I try and kick down the bed frame next. I guess I was making too much raucous because one of the nurses came in to stop me. He grabs me so tight and just hold me there commanding me to stop and calm down. I finally dissolve my anger into his arms. He asked that I come sit out in the hall with him.

"What is going through your head Mrs. Gilbert? Just earlier you were feeling fine and smiling."

"I had a dream, and it was loud. My body was shaking on the inside, while I was sleeping and I could not make it stop. I don't know if it the hallucinations again or what but I am tired. I am tired of these men thinking they can get over on me just because I am hot. I am married for Christ sake, there's no need for you or anyone else for that matter to come on to me. I AM MARRIED! EXIT THIS ROOM PLEASE."

He does exit, but within the minute a female nurse returns.

"I am going to tell you like I told him in hopes that because you bleed the same as me that you will understand. I have had everything stripped from me. I have been in this hospital for over more than enough week, and it is time that I leave. It is making me even more depressed to sit here and talk to you, because all you are going to do is go put it on my chart. I don't know what you guys are up to, but I am suing as soon as I get out of here, and I will get out. Even if I have to jump out the window, I will get out. Women are treated so brutally and are constantly dealing with the pressures of men. We get undressed with their eyes and expect to commit to all of their demands. What respect have I gained being in here? Let a man come in here, and tell you that he has been abused and sexually taken advantage of and you all will look at him strange, yet you will still command to his needs. Well picture me as a man and get me the hell up out of here."

CAN YOU KEEP A SECRET?

"Mam, there's no need to resort to dangerous measures. It is late and we are not prominent to allow patients to leave at this time."

My voice starts to crack, "I am in here day and night and the only feel of nature I get to view is from this stupid window. You guys do not even take patients outside while they are staying here. I understand some of us are crazy, I do. However, when we are showing improvement, there should be a reward for that, and the least you could do is hold their hand while they walk outside. I don't care if I am in chains to do so. I need to breathe, and you guys are suffocating the living death out of me. I am dead inside, can you feel that? I have danced with the devil himself, thinking that I would ever bleed for him. Are you kidding me, an you guys expect me to stay any longer? I've already gotten my proper medications. You can let me go now. That small out burst comes from being confined. Any much longer in here, I will not only find a way to hurt myself, but I will die on these discolored floors with my eyes open. You guys will see what I have went through, and hope to God it doesn't bother you in your sleep. Now do you really want my blood on your hands?"

CAN YOU KEEP A SECRET?

"Mrs. Gilbert, I apologize for any"

"Save it. Just get me out of here."

"As soon as possible Mrs. Gilbert, please get some rest. We'll see you in the morning."

"F@%# YOU!"

I try and sing myself to sleep. I start out with a hum and it doesn't sound the same, so I open my mouth a bit more. Nothing. My beautiful tone is gone. I have lost him.

I must save this woman. She is being man handled and captivated by what she believes is her true love. I go into their house to find her lying on the side of the bed ready to give up and end her life.

"C'mon I can help you", I say to her.

"There is no point Jah. He'll be back soon. Even if I leave from here, he will find me."

"I'm here, and I promise that will not happen. We can kill him before he gets too close."

"Do you really think we can? We are just woman of color. We're no match for his kind. We will be six feet under, even if we do succeed."

CAN YOU KEEP A SECRET?

I hear a car door slam. If we didn't leave now, we would have no chance to escape. We had to get to the car first. She drags around at first, but I give her some encouragement as we reached for the front window. She gets out first, and he recognizes her exit. Before he could get close to her, I jumped out the window nearly tripping over the pane and rush her to car door. We're in. I am in the driver's seat, while she took the back seat. He walks towards the car, picks up a brick and slams it through the front window. I've had enough of this monster. I put the car in drive and stomp on the gas, pushing him far back into the garage door. That wasn't enough. He must die right here at his own home. I back the car up a bit and stomp on the gas once more causing him to drop to his knees. He begs and pleas that he has had enough, but I haven't. I put the car in reverse once more and push as hard as I can on the gas. His head bashes against the wall leaving blood splattered all over the cement. I get out of the car and tell her to join me. I think she was coming down from her high because she was finally showing emotions.

"Well, you did it. Now what?"

"Let's dump him in the trash where he will remain until the police find him."

"Aren't you afraid of going to jail", she asks.

I woke up to the nurse grabbing my arm trying to take my vitals.

"You know now that you have awoken me, I won't be able to go back to sleep."

"Don't worry, breakfast will be served soon", the nurse replies.

I roll my eyes at her and cover my arms and face as she leaves. I can't believe I slept the whole night. They must be doing something right. The breakfast call comes over the intercom, and I decide to stay in my bed. They have seen enough of me. I lost my baby, so there's no need for me to try and force that bland ass food down my throat. Dr. Whitacker enters my room.

"I see that you have been sleeping Mrs. Gilbert. You're not causing anymore raucous, so I guess you will be on your way pretty soon."

CAN YOU KEEP A SECRET?

"How soon? Listen, I can't take much more of this place. Your nurses have kept me hear for nearly a month. I have not seen the broad of daylight yet."

"Yes, I know. Now if you are suicidal then we have to keep watch on you longer. Are you feeling the need to hurt yourself?"

"How many more bruises can I take. I am just ready to leave, so I will say any and everything just for you to acknowledge that I am fine."

"Okay Mrs. Gilbert. I understand. How are you liking your medications? Are they working for you? Do you feel any drowsiness, dizziness, or any abnormality during the day or night?"

"Pills are pills. I am able to sleep at night, so I guess something is working for me. I am always tired though even sitting here with you right now as though I have had plenty of sleep. The more that I talk to you about my problems, the more you are going to try to fix them correct? You are going to "keep watch" on me longer?"

"Well Mrs. Gilbert, if the side effects of the medications are too strong for you to handle, then I have to prescribe something that is more subtle on your mind."

"I'll be dead before morning."

"Please do not make comments like that Mrs. Gilbert unless you truly feel that way."

"You can leave now. I'll be here for when you get back."

"Please do, and I will see to get you the proper medications", he says as he walk out.

I figure I must get up and about and do something with my day. I walk into the tv room with my blanket, and everyone is staring at me in amazement. I pay them no mind and grab a seat at the table. I look up on tv to find my picture displayed on the news. It says that people ae in disbelief that a mother like me would be in the hospital after such tragic accident that happened with the daughter I didn't even know I had. News reporters are standing outside of the hospital giving their spill on such an "odd" occurrence. First, how do they even know I am here. Why does it matter that I don't know who that little girl is? They're calling me an unfit mother along with other traitorous names from the book of lies. They say a renowned lawyer like me should know better, and should not be causing such uproar within the hospital. Well, that is it for me. I could never go back to work after that. They are completely destroying everything that I have built. My sickness to them means nothing to them. They have turned me into a complete joke. I walk out of the room shaken up. I walk by the office and I see nurse Luanne smiling from the corner of my eye. She did this. Before I could get into my room, a familiar voice calls my name. It's my husband. I guess I care enough to go see what he has to say about all of this. I take a seat next to him in the room without the tv in it.

"How are you holding up", he says as if he is oblivious to everything that I once did to him.

"Not well. This place really has a system to it. One nurse told me that they keep people here based off false beliefs. I told her that if I do believe in God and she does not that that will keep me from walking away and seeing my family. Of course, she didn't want to get that technical, but that's what she meant."

"So you really believe you were pregnant?"

"I quenched at the smell of pizza and that is one of my favorite foods. I was nauseated the whole entire time and insides felt mushy and gullible all the time. It was like the only time I smiled was when I was by myself. I stayed in my room most of the time because that was the only thing that brought me peace. I had a voice that was so primitive that I sung everywhere I went just to calm my nerves. I thought of this place as my own show room. It was fun for a good little while. I know it sounds bazaar, but we did have sex the night I came in here, so it really isn't that far out. Because I know myself and can feel when my body changes, that makes my situational unbelievable if it is not findable. It cooked me for a while. I'm over it now. I just want to go home and lay in a real bed. I barely get any sleep here. When I do, I always come across the strangest dreams whether I am lighting up the world or saving another soul from being just as lost as I was. I am rediscovering myself all over again, being up in here babe."

"Well that is the first you have called me babe since I have been coming. Why have you neglected me?"

"I neglected myself hell and my needs. I couldn't stand to see anyone. I felt as if you were all to blame. I felt trapped. I mean how would you feel if you were screaming for someone to take your hand and say that they are on your side in the mist of everyone shutting your ideas down. You would feel great right? Well no one took my hand. Everybody broke every last one of my fingers the more I tried to reach out. I lost hope."

"So was I really to blame my love?"

"I guess not. It was mostly all in my head. I mean I have witness so many things in just my dreams alone. It was like I could never get out of that realm or experience. I always felt like I had to fight for something or someone. I was on a whole other frequency of spirits. My mind took me places and had me think that I was someone else. Maybe I was though. I just could never put the two realities together. No one understood the way I talked. Most people round here would say that I was possessed or jabbering off at the mouth one. I question that side of me still to this day. I have not figured out exactly what the other world was trying to tell me. Maybe you can help me decipher it a little more. I know it's out of your speed, but what I felt inside me was far from supernatural. I was invincible to say the least."

"How do you feel now?"

That's a good question. The meds are constantly having me loopy or drowsy. I feel like I am always high or floating. When I sleep, well you know that part. I walk around here just like everybody else, waiting for something interesting to happen. The tv is a blur. I could never get my mind to focus on it long enough without thinking that they are talking about me. At one point I would believe that I was conversing with the talk show host through my mind and letting her in to some secrets I was hiding that she so told abstractly. This is my life now. I wouldn't say that I am confused. I think I am more so broken and have reach my last tipping point."

"What has broken you?"

"You put a smile on my face with every one of your questions. I like them. I truly do. It makes me feel important to you and feels as if you really care about my sense of being. I'm not real sure on what has broken me. Though if I was to get a shot at it, I would say my dreams. I never shared this part of my life with you. I don't know why. I just figured it would be better kept a secret that I wouldn't have to relive. When I was about thirteen years old, I aspired to be a professional model. With years of hard work, by the age of fifteen I was able to get signed with one of the biggest modeling agency in history, FORD MODELS MIAMI. It was great at first, traveling to different cities and meeting new people. However, not all people were good. It was this one photographer down in Miami that did a shoot for me. I was literally on my last leg with this one because all of my hair fell out, and I had to cut it. My hair, my face, and my body are what booked me gigs. One without the other was just unfit. My agent, which was like the best of them all, she took me to get a whole new due. Some would say that my haircut was a Grace Jones due. I guess they were trying to make me legendary. Anyway, the photographer was the first to see after my cut. A new look meant a new image, and a new image meant new updated pictures. This photoshoot was like no other because I had to get undressed in front of camera. Now I was eighteen by this time, so it was totally legal. As one piece of clothing came off after the next, I saw the photographer stop to look at me every few takes. He said that what I was doing with my eyes in the camera made him feel as if we had some sort of chemistry. I was not very translucent with my words, so I quickly smiled in hopes that we could get the pictures done so I could leave as soon as possible. After we shot one scene, we went down to the beach side to do more photos. Taking my clothes off and on left me feeling ridiculous. I wasn't that comfortable with my body anyway even when being a size 2.

CAN YOU KEEP A SECRET?

While at the beach, the photographer would hold up a towel in front of me, so that I could soon get undressed and be ready to shoot again. While I was taking off my panties, I felt his eyes on my body. I glanced up to find him directly staring at my vagina. As if I wasn't uncomfortable enough, I still went with it. Anything for the shot right. We took the photos on the sand and then wrapped up the shoot. It was until days later where my agent saw the photos in disbelief. She didn't like a single one, and I couldn't blame her. She asked me what was wrong or what I might have being going through, since it is unlike me to take such unnatural photos. I couldn't speak on my experience for some reason. I guess my time was up. I haven't done another photoshoot since. I guess that was part of my breakage point. I always had to appear perfect. Perfect hair, perky boobs, nice curves, every day in high school I was some public figure to the human eye. No one ever knows what goes on behind the scenes of perfection, and quite frankly most don't have the time to listen. I never really shared this story with anyone, not even my mom. I had to get it out though. I loved my job as a model. Though the more I got older, the more my features changed, and people were starting to look at me and my body as a grown woman. I wasn't though. I was still learning, and I am still learning being 27 today. What do you say though to a person who has your dreams in the palm of their hands."

"You can say no sometimes babe. You can."

"I know that now."

"Well thanks for sharing. I'm going to head out now", Vincent says as he gets up.

I look at him in awe.

"I'm just kidding babe. I would never leave you after you sharing something like that or for any period for that matter. I just had to break the ice a little bit. It was getting pretty toasty in here", he says with a smile.

"Thanks for not leaving me. I didn't even know I had that in me. I've been keeping it bottled up for so long that I forgot that it was unresolved."

"Do you feel that is resolved now?"

"I do. I have gotten it off my chest. Maybe I will stop having these ferocious dreams now."

"Would you like for me to explain this to the doctor?"

"Please", I reply.

"Cool. I think it is my time to go now, they are signaling the last call. Call me if you need me, and I will be here to pick you up as soon as they release you. I'll explain everything to your mother as well. I know she would have an ear for this."

"Thank you. You truly are a great husband. Maybe I'll start to uncover more secrets a little later."

"Oh, so you have more to tell?"

"I have more to tell. One day though babe. One day. "

I walk back to my room feeling lighter and in control. Man, that felt good. Who knew all of that was inside of me. There are wonders of the world that the mind can only process when it is healthy. Maybe those pills are doing a little something. I feel great, and I am starving. I wish I hadn't skipped breakfast, but I know lunch is going to be marvelous. I can feel it.

Sitting in my room, I look outside to see the sun shinning through the window. Man, if they didn't have windows, this place would truly suck. I guess it gives you an extra push to stay alive. My days here are winding down. I can feel that too. The nurse comes in with my morning medication. I'm glad it was not Luanne. If it was, I might would have had to cut her or at least let her endure what I was going through seeing my face plastered every where in the news. No matter though. The talk with my husband gave me great satisfaction that might last me through the entire rest of my stay. I have gotten a lot off my chest and my mind, so no one can harm my words that much. I feel way better than I did when I came in here, and I know I probably look different too. I take my meds with pleasure. Soon enough the doctor will come back and decipher my pills and hopefully relieve me. I take a knee beside my bed to talk to God a little bit more.

I have felt your spirit come over me numerous of times, but today I feel it exceptionally more. Thank you for not allowing me to go to far under my self-control and lose my sense of ability to stand. I am now better, and able to establish who I am, under your world, is incompetence to who you are Lord God. I apologize for trying to strike myself, hold my breath, and cause madness to those around me. I haven't decided on what I am going to do, when I get out of here, but leaving is a start. I pray that you will help me with the rest. I also want to apologize to my mother and father for making them feel as if they are unwanted in my life. I never meant to hurt anybody or myself for that matter. I won't play victim anymore, instead I come to you as a humble spirit and ask for forgiveness. I hope that you will pass this message on to my family, or give me the strength to say it to them myself one day. I don't think I want to go back to my old life anymore, yet I don't want to start over. It is like I want to begin a new journey from where I left it and complete my aspirations. It has to have something to do with my culture and the people that walk this earth blind/ unaware of their inner self. We are all connected, and I would like for others to see that as well. I pray that you gather my mind together first and make me whole again. I can't bare going to church anymore. The thought of someone yelling in my ear and writing all of my wrongs is not fair. I would be looked at as an outcast, even though I come as I are. The members are so contradicting sometimes, but I know I am not there for them. Maybe one day I will return but just to visit. I can't be in one place for too long. I feel conformed and shallow, if I stay, because I am forever changing. How can one book define me and pick me to pieces, when the trees out in the open don't even grow the same way every day. It is not that I am going against your word. I just don't perceive one book with a fixed set of rules as your holy word. Some things in it, however, are relatable. I just don't want to become stuck or close minded from following a ritual that you have not designed for myself. I have not found your direction for me just yet, but I know you are there. I need your help God, and I don't want to go to anybody but you. If you lead me to someone, then I will follow. In hopes to be relieve from this hole soon, I'll see you in my dreams. Thanks for the talk. Amen.

I get up and lie back down on my bed day dreaming of sweet nothings and new beginnings. I am so powerful with my words, sometimes I think I could possibly be a motivational speaker. I know I wouldn't make as much as my career now as a lawyer, but I want to put the money aside for now and find a purpose. I am given the breath of life every day, and I waste it on myself. I want to do more than just write up contracts and give my opinion. I want to give facts of the new world and the declaration of nature's energy. Even if I do not make any money, I will be doing more than wonders to spread onto the world. I know that day is coming, so I won't force it.

"Mrs. Gilbert, I have good news. I will be releasing you today on account of your good behavior and your proper response to the medication. They seem to be working, and you are talking normal. There is no need to keep you here any longer. Are you ready?", Dr. Whittaker says to me.

"Well, I rather not get sassy with you might keep me here longer. I'll save my answer. Yes, I am more than ready to leave."

"Okay, let me gather your notes and paper work and send your information over to Behavioral Health. I won't even ask you if you have enjoyed your stay. Promise me you will better yourself, once you leave out these doors. Oh, and please take your medication, every day. I don't want to see you back in here Mrs. Gilbert."

"It's not like you all can deal with me anyways. Thank you though, I am ready to see my family outside of this hole."

Vincent comes to pick me up as he said he would, and the first thing I would like to have is frozen yogurt and a nice juicy burger. As soon as I walk out the hospital doors, a reporter bum rushes me with a camera.

CAN YOU KEEP A SECRET?

"How does it feel to finally be out of the mental institution?", she asks.

Well she surely wanted to make known of where I was at for the past month in a half.

"I rather not speak to you, if that is okay with you. I must get going."

"Will you be attending your daughter's funeral? Are you upset with your husband for cheating?", she proceeds to ask.

I walk away with my head held high. She or crusty ass Luanne is not going to ruin my moment. I'm going to go eat some good food, and I don't care who sees. I have had a great talk with God, and I am out of my dilemma. A few words can't hurt.

Vin takes me home to change and fix up my face. On the car ride home, he asks me would I like for him to explain the whole daughter issue. I tell him I don't care at this point and my mind isn't well rested enough for me to have a decent conversation with good commentary to add. He agrees with me. Taking all of these sightings in is kind of new to me. The air looks fresher than when I last saw it, and the roads are more balanced. The buildings are still tall and beautifully mimicking the trees' body. Vincent stops by one of the nearby stores to fill up his tank and leaves me in the car. To tell you the truth, I don't care to interact with the world just yet. I rather remain invisible until I am comfortable. I see a man out of the corner of my eye walking towards the car and I panic. I immediately lock the doors and sink back down into the seat. What is going on with me, I think to myself. All of a sudden, I am scared and nervous about what nature put out onto this earth. He walks pass the truck and I thank God. I don't know what it is. I feel like everyone is out to get me or wants something from me. This must be that new awareness from being locked up for so long. It would be nice, if the nurses took the patients out every now and again. We probably won't be so threaten by the world once we enter it again. All I know is that I would like for my husband to be back by my side again.

He hops back into the truck and I tell him to please never leave my side. I've been alone for too long. He suggested that maybe I should stay with my mother for a while, so someone can watch me while he is at work. He may be on to something with that one.

CAN YOU KEEP A SECRET?

We make it home, and I dart for the shower. How nice to feel something hot on my body, rather than luke warm. It indeed feels nice. As it hits my body, I close my eyes and all of the memories from the hospital start to playback in my head. I gasp for air, as if I forgot that the water was pouncing down onto my face. I stand on the side of the shower for a bit. They say dreams will scare you, but what about memories? They, too, are powerful. I quickly wash down and turn off the water. I step out to face the mirror and wipe away the fog with my hands. She looks different. Her hair is filled with new growth and is as long as her arms and legs. I haven't aged a bit. My features just appear stronger. My cheekbones have taken shape, and my face has sunken it. I lost a lot of weight that I don't even recognize myself anymore. I drop the towel to look at the rest of my body. My breasts are heavier, and my stomach has a pudge. My hips have spread, yet my thighs are still the same with maybe a little bit more definition. I pick up my towel and wrap myself back up. I go into our bedroom and even this feels foreign. I lock the door and lie the towel down in one spot. I climb onto the bed and lie flat on the towel. Mmmm, now this feels normal. What an experience to be there for so long. Vin knocks on the door. I get up, wrap myself in the towel to open the door. A whiskey burger with bacon and fried onions with pepper jack cheese melted on to it from Applebees just how I like it. He hands the tray over to me, smiles, and closes the door. He must be magic because I don't remember him leaving. He may have gotten it ordered to our front door. It's here now, and I can't wait to dive into it.

I lay back in awe of what is melting inside of my mouth. The thought of me being home and fully relaxing and not having to answer to anyone's bucking call or alarm. God I am so appreciative, and I apologize for any ungrateful acts I have caused in the past. I'm here now, and I promise to be present. Vincent comes in and sits on the bed with me. I get under the covers with my towel.

"Do you think I'll be like this forever?", I ask him.

"What do you mean? Your state of mind?"

"Yeah, like will I have to take medicine for the rest of my life?"

"Depends if you stop smoking that tree", he laughs.

"Yeah and stop making love to you too huh?"

"That wasn't funny."

CAN YOU KEEP A SECRET?

"Neither was your joke", I say with a smile.

"I don't know babe. Maybe not. That's not important right now though. We just got to get you back on your feet."

"And we will. Let's turn the focus on you now. Who is this child I know nothing about, and why don't I know anything about her?"

"It was before I met you. I didn't know she was pregnant until years later this little girl calls my phone calling me daddy. I thought it was a joke, so I didn't too much respond. However, her mom, Zora, came to my office with the little girl telling me that she is mine."

"Are you sure she is yours?"

"I remembered messing around with Zora in college. It was so brief that I didn't think anything of it, plus the little one looks exactly like me features and all. I'm so sorry I didn't tell you. I thought I could pay her off and leave that in my past."

"Well why didn't you tell me?"

"We have such a good thing. I didn't want you to worry, and well now you don't have to since you know."

"How could you say that? She was your seed! She came from you, and all of this time I've been wanting my very own child. Why? Why couldn't I have had one of yours? Except I had to sacrifice my embryo to save my own damn life to have you sit up here and tell me that you didn't even want to be in her life? What kind of nonsense is that Vin? You didn't even want to see her or even watch her grow up. Now I'm sitting in the hospital defending your stupid…I thought you wanted kids."

"Not with her.

"But you lied down in the bed with her and that was a choice of yours. She was obviously good enough for you to leave your seed in her. All of those times we talked about how men should respect woman and how women should hold men accountable for their actions because we are the wind of the earth. What was that? You know how to talk that good good 'til you get in and good. Then, all of the chivalry goes down the drain. You can leave now. I left the hospital not too long ago, and I am trying to enjoy my freedom, instead I'm listening to you plead a sorry case. Please leave, and take a pillow and blanket with you."

"As you wish", he replies.

CAN YOU KEEP A SECRET?

This is ridiculous. Why now, and why did it have to be true? I turn over and try to get some sleep, but the thought of him having his first child with a woman he cold careless about, rather than with his wife who has fought for her unborn child all by herself. No one believed me. I could have met his daughter and took her places. "Could of should of would of right?" Yeah whatever. If it ain' one thing it's another. Good thing I am on my meds because I would have spazzed on him so bad. Might would have me locked up or in the insane asylum now fighting for a young lady I never got to meet. Ironic.

I'm in a game that I have designed, yet I do not know my way out. The rolling ball captures me in its hole and we roll up the track. I can't identify who is in the seat next to me, but it is someone close to me. I am not able to see his/her face. We roll up the coast and have a face off to see who can exit first. The ball will turn into gas if we do not get out in time. I struggle to squeeze my way through the ball. My arms reach out over the ball and I push myself up with my legs, kicking the other guy in his face. I jump up and enter this black hole, and I soar. Flying beside this poll, I feel a disconnect and I soon start to fall thousands of feet from above. Scared as I might be, I keep my eyes in front of me without looking down. I can feel the bottom reaching closer. I fall straight down and land on my two feet. I look up astonished and thank God for my landing. The crowd, in the theater, is in tears. What just happened?

Chapter 12

Her hair comes down to her shoulders, and it has some bounce to it. Her eyes are spaced out then normal. There's some attraction to her, but I can't pin point it yet. She dresses very poise unlike myself, where as I put on the earth. She's sitting down at one of the outside tables with her legs crossed reading what seems to be an intimate book. Her facial expressions tell it all. I walk up to her very gently. I don't want to startle her.

"Hi, I'm Jahanna. Zora right?"

"In the flesh. Nice to finally meet you", she says to me.

"You say it like you have been waiting to meet me all this time."

"Well, I have, but only because of what has been swirling in the news. I am not here to disrupt your family. I know having a miscarriage must be difficult, so I wanted to help ease the pain by sharing my daughter with you. I brought baby pictures and all. It might actually give you a better view on who Neil was."

"Her name is Neil?"

"Yes. I'm one to keep family names going, so I named her after her grandfather. Do you like it?"

"I love it. It is quite unique. What was she like?"

"Neil loved the outdoors. She went to a camp for girls ever since she was old enough to. She had a passion for people. Neil felt like she had to inspire the world some way with her voice."

"She sung?"

"Did she! She couldn't stop singing. She sung every scripture of the bible as if it was a love song. She was a true believer. Neil believed in any and everything. She would take heights with her grandfather all the time. She had this connection to nature that was inseparable."

"What did she want out of life?"

"She didn't have so much of an interest to school as others, but she did very well in it. Neil wasn't your average gal. From the pictures, you can definitely tell she was heavy set. Her weight inspired her first. Neil would tell me all the time that the picture of the human world was filled with neglections of the natural human body. She was no model, and she wasn't trying to be. Neil wanted to be a role model first. She would talk of such things at such a young age that I thought she needed to be on someone's stage or in someone's program teaching and inspiring the youth the real picture of love. Here's some of her practice speeches she wrote late at night in her room. The funny thing is that I had to always force her to go to bed, or she would be up all night rambling on with her spirit."

I looked at her pictures and speeches. She for sure looks like Vincent, and her speeches are remarkable. She reminds me much of myself the way she talked about feminism, self-love, and even depression. That term stuck out to me most.

"So, was Neil going through a state of depression?", I asked her mother.

"That's where you come in. I know you were in the hospital for deepened depression. I never would have expected Neil to be depressed because her everlasting enthusiasm to change the world. However, not knowing her dad would mess with her from time. It was like she could never settle with anyone because they were never good enough."

"Which she shouldn't have to being at how young she was."

"Very true, but there was this one guy that had her head spinning all of the time. She kept him hidden for at least three years, according to her journal. He was part of some gang, and she felt the need to be by his side all of her time. It says here

183

that they spent all of summer 2014 together just riding around making hits throughout the city. I just don't see how she ended up with such a guy that is complete opposite of her demeanor. She wrote so many poems about him and her drawings were so disturbing."

"Was she on any substance that might have altered her state of mind?"

"Not that I am aware of, but it does say that the guy smoked heavy marijuana. She might have tried it, but I never recognized any signs when she would walk through the house. The further I read into her diary though, the more I am confused. It starts to jump from month to month and to these dreams that she can't decipher."

"She had dreams too?"

"You are a dreamer?"

"Well kind of, they come and go and they are never the same. I don't know what to really call them anymore."

"What has the doctor's said about them?"

"I haven't really discussed that part with them. While I was in the hospital, I wanted much to myself. They took my freedom. All I had left was.well my mind."

184

CAN YOU KEEP A SECRET?

"Did you ever write these feelings down?"

"While I was in there, no. However, I did keep a journal like your daughter Neil. Except my journal was pretty straight forward. I never had distorted thoughts when writing in it."

"What do you think? Neil kept such a private life hidden from me, and I have no idea why", her mother said.

"Do you think that she would ever harm herself?"

"You were thinking the same huh? The police say the accident could have possibly been a suicide. I'd hate to think that, but it seems she was crying out for help and I couldn't see it."

"Well you can't blame yourself. It is not like you saw the signs and ignored them. She was acting and presenting herself to you in a normal way every time she walked into the house. What else could you inspect?"

"I don't know, but as a mother it's different. I heard on the news that you were pregnant as well?"

"The doctors didn't want to believe it because my pregnancy did not show up on their test. I could feel it though. I don't know what it was that gave me such confirmation, but I felt it deep in my spirit. I sacrificed my child though to save my health. There was no way I could keep her. She was having me do all sorts of things. I was acting out of turn and calling everyone out of their name. It was like the child was destroying me but keeping me alive at the same time. I knew once I started taking those pills the doctor prescribe, I couldn't keep her. It was either let her live, prove everyone wrong, and have her coming out of me dysfunctional or let go and get better."

"How did you sacrifice her?"

"I prayed."

"Do you think my daughter and yours could have had some connection?"

"I was thinking that, but I didn't want to freak you out."

"Listen, after reading my daughter's journal, my mind is fully awoken to as many possibilities as there are. Neil was fearless, and she didn't care what anyone thought of her."

"What made her grow dreadlocks?"

"It was all her. She said it was liberating to listen to her hair, and let it do what it wants without transforming it under control. I tell ya, you never knew what to expect from her or what came out of Neil's mouth. She read so many books that you simply could not get her to stop talking."

CAN YOU KEEP A SECRET?

We both started laughing.

I found it empowering for Zora to share this information. She could have been like the rest and ignore me completely. Maybe Neil and I were more connected then I thought. It certainly must be devastating to go through this alone, but she keeps a smile on her face for some reason.

"How do you feel about your daughter's death?", I asked her in the politest way I could.

"Where ever she is now, I know that she is more happy than she was when walking this earth. There is more life where she is now, and I know she is having a blast exploring different realms of life. I still think that she will come back to me in some kind of form. I was sad and upset at first with how she handled things. She wasn't angered when she left the house. I don't know why she took the car, Neil doesn't even have her license. It's not like I could do anything about her leaving. Like I have stated before, I don't know what was going through her head. Maybe that's just how she wanted things to go. I don't know, but can we talk about something else for a while. I don't want to draw tears today. It's beautiful outside, and I know she is looking down on me. She wouldn't want me to worry. I still feel her presence. I don't think that feeling will ever depart, considering the fact that she was my daughter. I don't mind it though. How are things with you and Vincent. I heard you knocked him out, while you were in the hospital. What was that like. Hell, I don't blame you. You did it for you and me."

"I don't know what came over me to tell you the truth. I guess I felt that he could have done more to save me. Him visiting me in the hospital all the time was kind of like a slap in the face. Of course, he is my husband, and he is going to do the matron things. I felt disconnected to him the whole time I was there though. He's a good guy I suppose. I turned everyone away. I didn't want any phone calls or nothing. I was the only one that believed in my pregnancy, so I guess I felt alone."

"Was there any part of your stay that was enjoyable?"

"I was there for over a month, of course I had to find something but there was nothing there to cling to. I even tried to take my own life by shortening my breath from time to time, or destroy things that were in my reach."

"How do you feel now that you are out into the free world?"

"I feel free I guess. I get to eat whatever I want. That's a plus. You really can't appreciate someone or the things in this "free world" if you haven't had all of your rights and possessions stripped from you. I'm not going back I can tell you that much."

"What are you going to do about your career? You say you are a lawyer, right?"

"I could sue and win hahaha. No, but I think I'm going to take a little time for myself and do the things I love, rather than to be subjected to something that doesn't hold my interest. I want to go on more hikes, swim more, sky dive, and talk to the birds more. If I can't have the things that I would like to see happen, well I might as well create it right?"

"It sounds like you need to write a book."

"Funny you are. Who knows, however, I have to get myself together first. I was just like Neil at one point. Writing for no reason and flowing so comfortably with the change of seasons that I forgot how to be myself. I got lost in my writings. Can you believe that? It was so easy to lose sight of what's real."

"And what is real to you Ms. Jahanna?"

"Love. That's what really makes the world go around. The love for money, or the love for intangible objects, it all compares to nothing in the end. It is the love, however, that keeps everything afloat. That is why no matter the change of seasons, we are still moving towards the sight of love."

"You should take trips with your husband and fall in love with him again. Love may help."

"If you say so dear. It is not that I don't love him. I believe it is more of me trying to find his spirit somewhere in the vibration of my heart beat. I love him though. We've been together for this long. I must love him for something right? I won't hold you up no longer though. I know you have to prepare for Neil's burial and things of that sort. It was a really nice dive into this conversation we have had. I will pray for you in hopes to one day see you again. I know it might be too forward to actually try and hang out with you, but I definitely will pray for you."

"And thank you for respecting my boundaries. I enjoyed this conversation as well. It made me feel a little better about the situation. The fact that you and Neil are so closely related, I certainly would love to see you again. When the tide presents itself, of course.

I drive back home listening to soft melodies to clear my mind. My spirit feels clean, and I can't wait to talk to my journal, when I get home. I know my hubby is probably worried sick about me. I'll stop by my mom's house though to at least give her the greatest hug there is. It is a good thing we stay a block away from them. I know she'll have a home cooked meal waiting for me. She always puts the best spices into her secret sauces. Mothers have this secret way about them that only they can be loved for. I guess that's why I was so hip to having my own. To feel the love of bliss is indescribable no matter what anyone tried to discredit me for. No matter. That is neither here nor there. I'm out now, and I can't wait to see my small little family.

"Where have you been Mrs. Gilbert", Vin asks as I creep into the door.

"I spoke with Zora today. She has such a kind spirit. I can't see why you would just leave her in the dust to take care of Neil by herself."

"She has plenty of money okay, and I took well care of her every month. She wasn't suffering."

"But maybe Neil was."

"How do you figure that?"

"You never saw her I'm guessing, and she was in search for you for quite some time. How could you just leave them two to fend for themselves and not know that Neil would some day grow up to want a father to hold her and squeeze all of her pain away?"

"It's much harder to explain."

"Is it? But it was much easier to do right?"

"I was young."

"But you got older, and you still resisted to see her. You know she was going through a depressed state like I was. Mixing her emotions with guys that could care two cents about her because her father was never there to say the words 'I love you', how do you explain that? You can't, and you expect me to be okay with that and say that it is water under the bridge. You should talk to Zora, or at least read Neil's diary. It might not have been your fault to the reason why I was in the hospital. It was surely yours though, when it comes to Neil. She practically let her self go thinking that she would be better off in another world, and in the arms of her savior that could protect her from anything or anyone such as yourself. I don't get it. I mean I really don't understand how you end someone's life like that. Neil wanted you!"

I left him with the impression that I was mad until he can find an explanation for his actions. I start to prepare his dinner even though I have already eaten. I'm still his wife right? I have to accept the good and the bad of our marriage. Damn those vows, but I will accept the change for now. I go into our room and write a bit in my journal.

Wow, it feels so good to touch you again and hold you close. I have so much to tell you, but in the same instance nothing at all. I'll start with the sense of why men are so greedy. They are in the need of us more than we are of them. You would think that one woman man is ideal, but they always seem to need more. Once before, Vincent asked me if I would ever go for an open relationship. I was willing to give it some thought, but that was only because I have love for him. What happens when the other woman gets attached, or the other woman will not leave? Women are crazy about men, and I am questioning what that is all about. I love my husband and I am crazy myself. However, I don't think I would ever go crazy over my man because I have done it so many times before. It is simply too much energy to stress over a man that doesn't want to settle. Love is a force, but it is not forced. If my man wanted to go, I would gladly show him the door. Of course, I may hurt a bit and debate about his existence, but I would soon over come it. My answer to Vin was no. If I can't complete you, then I don't want any missing pieces dangling around my home. I am not here to just cook and clean, while he goes out and try to build stones out of dirt. The interesting thing about this "open relationship" thing is that the woman can never be as equal to the man. By this I mean that I would not be able to do the same thing as Vin in return. I don't know journal. Men are strange. Vincent has surely change over the years now that I am married to him, and I wouldn't expect anything less. It's practically unjust and unfit some of the things he says to me. I think I need to get a way, maybe have a trip with my girls. It would do me right to go to a place where no one can find me, and it is only the girls and I. I would like that, so let's make that happen journal. Come with, yes?

Chapter 13

I meet up with my girls the next day, and they were thinking the same. Tired of their men, the double standards, and the ambiguity in their voices. We decide on a trip to California. We wasted no time in buying the tickets. The hotel we are staying at is beautiful and has a nice view. Our plane leaves at 9am on Thursday. We have tons of fun shopping and playing around for the trip. We invite our good friend Nia to join because her sass is undeniable. Everyone has a different personality. Shay is good with directions and finding the live spots. Brooke is up for anything and always bring good booze. Nia, well we all know of her. Then there is me with nothing but trouble to bring to the group. It's quite funny how we all match up. We go into this clothing store where there is nothing but bathing suits all around us. It's like walking on air, when coming into the store. Everyone decides on different set pieces to decorate their body with. I went for the one piece because I have a wide load behind me, and a two piece cannot hold up this storage no matter how tight the strings are.

"How does this look?", Brooke says.

"Like you are about to go for a jog", I replied.

"So, what you are saying is this isn't cute?"

"To say the least."

"Why didn't you just start with that? Never mind, let me try on another."

I guess I was the judge of the different suits today because all of the rooms were filled, and I was left to stand outside. Nia is probably the easiest to decide on what to wear. She didn't try on many, and every single one she loved no matter anyone else opinion. Now Shay, she was the hardest. Nothing ever lied on her body the way that she would have liked.

"Woah, that one is cute girl. You should get it", Nia says to Shay.

"Yeah, but my boobs are way too big for this suit. They are suffocating under this top. I can't."

"You still want it to be sexy though."

"Yeah but not uncomfortable."

"How uncomfortable is it really because that is really cute?"

"A ten out of ten for sure."

"Well if you don't get, then I might have to."

CAN YOU KEEP A SECRET?

Shay takes it off in a hurry and hands it over to Nia. We all bust out laughing. Brooke finally finds one that doesn't make her look like she's training for the Olympics. Great now I can go try on my three, and I bet you I will make a faster decision than them.

That was fun to say the least. I really don't enjoy things riding up my spine that much. We all are dying of hunger from shopping all day. We aren't as naïve as we were, when we were younger. Instead of going out to eat, we save our money for the trip and go home and cook what is at the house. Even though I really don't want to go home, I go anyway for the sake of I am tired.

I get home and head for the shower first. There is something about having hot water now that I am so infatuated with. It sounds silly, and Vincent is always making fun of me for it. He asks if he could join. I guess I don't mind. He gets in too quick and nearly makes a slip. He grabs on to me, and I start laughing. He smiles and says that he is happy I am smiling now. According to him, ever since I have been out the hospital, I have been a little more snarky than normal. He starts fiddling with my hands and interlocks his with mine. He wraps his arms around my waist and just holds me. He squeezes me real tight just like he used to do before I would close my eyes to sleep. As he holds me, Vin starts to shuffle his feet around very slowly as if he wants me to follow his lead. There is no music going on, but I can feel his rhythm.

"I'm sorry."

"For what exactly?"

"For everything. I didn't mean for anyone to get hurt, when I made the decision that I made. I wasn't stable at the time, and I thought it was better for Zora if I left."

"But you even said.."

"Those were past aggressions from my own fault. I didn't know how to be a man. I was too caught up in my own world to even think of a child. I was wrong, and I was more wrong to leave them with cluttered head. I've made my wrongs, and now I am trying to rewrite them. Sending money every month is no match for physical appearances. I know that now. As cliché as it sounds, I met you and all of those wrongs didn't matter anymore. I wanted to start over and be a better man. One day I knew I would visit Neil, but I kept telling myself I wasn't ready and that she would reject me. Since I couldn't spend time with her, while she was alive, I went to her grave sight and left a letter underneath the flowers. I know the flowers will fade, and the letter will soon blow away. However, I know she is out there somewhere running around as free as she can be. Maybe she will read it in her spare time."

"It's certainly a start.'

"I don't expect you to forgive me right away."

"But I do."

"Why?"

"Why not. There is no sense in putting you down, when you have seen your greatest disappointment fall right below your eyes. You were wrong, of course. I was also mad. I'm not anymore. Neil resembled natures alignment so much that she blends right in with her spirit. I know she is safe, and I know she is exactly where she wants to be. She'll come visit you when she wants, or she may never. You tried and that is enough. At least she never wanted for anything. I want to be just like her when I grow older. I do need some time away from you though. My plane leaves tomorrow morning. Thank you, nonetheless, for this conversation. Have a date planned for me when I get back. We haven't done much together in a while. I want to fall in love with you again. I have missed you."

"I'm right here."

"No, you are not."

We wash each other off. He tries to get sexual with me, but I stop him. Vincent is a nice guy, and I know that he can be a great man. I just need him to try a little harder every now and again. This is not the time to become complacent and stagnant. I need him to step up his greatness and cherish the wife he sees before his eyes. A little tough love doesn't hurt. A God-fearing man is what I need. I need him to get back to that because God is the only being holding us upright.

Thursday

"C'mon! We're going to be late", I say as we all dart for the closing doors. Brooke and I woke up late. Nia kept calling, but no one would answer the phone. It was kind of funny seeing us run around like we had our head cut off. Shay kept tripping over her bag. Nia brought too many bags. As for me, I only had one carry on. Brooke on the other hand got to the door before all of us.

"Wait don't close the doors! My friends are coming down the hall!", she shouts.

We all made it there in time before the lady could even say no. It was much like sardines found there way to the ocean the way we pilled up against Brooke. Shay tripped over her bag again and threw it on the ground in frustration. I told her to hand it to the lady. This way she wouldn't have to worry about the stupid thing anymore. We all laugh hysterically at Shay, as we walk on up to the plane. However, if we missed the plane, then everyone will be looking shameful. What a great way to start our girls' trip.

Everyone gets to their seats. Surprisingly, we all are sitting in close range of one another. Shay and Brooke immediately call the flight attendant over for some drinks. We all needed to relax, but I didn't want to fall asleep. I wanted to enjoy the scenery all much of what there was, so I only had a glass of wine.

"Yal act like yal tensed or something the way you all are throwing them shots back", I say to them with a giggle.

Nia went straight to sleep as soon as she got on the plane, so no worries for her. Brooke and Shay just look at me with a rhetorical face expression. It was a decent trip, so I took out a book that I picked up from Goodwill and started to read it in the meantime. It was much of a supernatural book and gave women universal gifts to fight back predators. My only gift is my mouth. I say what I feel all the time. Sometimes it is too blunt for most, but it will get clogged in my chest if I never let it come out. I think that is why I am so hard on my husband. I just expect so much from him, but I never hear him out fully. If it is not what I want to hear, then for the majority, I turn my nose to it. It's a good thing I brought my journal. This book will settle me for now. Hopefully Darcy can keep it under control for the rest of the flight.

We have arrived, and the drunks are far from sober. I don't even think that they know where they are or how they got to LAX. Nia and I laugh at them and the messy state that they are in.

"C'mon yal. We can't stay on the plane forever. Don't forget to grab your wig Shay."

"Such a hater you are, darling", she says as she grabs for it.

We step onto the Californian ground and it feels so surreal. It's nothing like Georgia. I can tell you that much. The air smells different. It's like a fresh Dove scent, but in nature form. We grab our luggage from baggage claim, and search for the car rental place. Brooke is the only one that is from here, so she finds it with ease. I was in charge of getting the car, so I ended up getting us a nice utility vehicle that could fit all of our bags in. The first stop is the hotel because we have got to get out of these sweats. We checked in. This was to be our stay for the next couple of days. Nia and I go explore the hotel a little bit, while Shay and Brooke rest their heads some more. It was nice to see a change. Everything so formal yet relaxed. We saw that they had an open bar off to the left. There was a mini club inside the hotel as well. It covered the back of the hotel. They also had a theater and ballroom to lounge around in. Nia and I go sit at the bar for a savory glass of wine.

"So, what's your next move? I know you have been singing for a while now and promoting your own business. Do you plan on taking it next level?"

"I don't know you know. I really would like to move to the city. I mean California is beautiful. Maybe I'll try ATL first though. I really would like to be a motivational speaker more than singing. Singing is just a release for me. Don't get me wrong, I'm great at it, but I feel I can reach people on a higher platform", she says to me.

"I think that is wonders. You have the same drive that I have now. Yes, I make tons of money studying law. However, it isn't fulfilling as much as I thought it was going to be. With my degree, I protect people. Now I would like to change it around and listen to people and hear their concerns of the free world. We protect the problems of people, but we don't do anything about it except cut them a check. There must be more to life than just money. That's why I wanted to come out here. I needed a different perspective, and this is right up my alley."

"Do you think you and Vincent will move to a place like this?"

"Ideally, I would love to. I captured the energy as soon as I step foot unto its soil. I don't know if I could do Atlanta so much."

"Yeah it's way too crowded."

"Exactly."

"I came out here to open my mind a little more on what direction I wanted to take with my business. I'm thinking maybe I can buy some land out here to expand my ideas. How is your medication treating you? I know you gave the doctors hell for having to take it."

"The medication is cool. It has me high all of the time, so I am eating more and more each day. I think I'll get it replaced one of these days. It is helping me control my thoughts better. With a racing mind filling up your time, you need something to keep you grounded."

"Do you believe that is why you were hallucinating in your dreams?"

CAN YOU KEEP A SECRET?

"Well, I smoke some marijuana before I entered the hospital. Some people say it is harmless. When you have an enlightened mind and you initially do not look at the world as it is presented, putting a rooted plant that came from the earth into your system elevates you to an even higher frequency. I believe that is why everyone reacts differently to it. The feeling that I experience is like sticking your feet in a tub of ice water after running three miles without stopping. It's enticing yet it strikes your nerves making everything in your body turn black. There was no escape door or vent I could breathe through. I was covering my thoughts with the sight of love. They were unraveling so fast, I started to put them in substitute of the silence that I felt in my heart. I knew I was loved, but I couldn't trigger that emotion. Instead it came out in a state of me altering my conscience. That time has passed. I still have flashbacks, and I don't remember some of things I said or did. Vincent helps me with that part."

"You're so brave Jah, especially to come to California only days after your release from the hospital. If you ever need to talk more, I am here. I don't want you to ever feel in alone in this mayhem that you have experienced."

"Okay, now can we go wake those two up and get our day started. I'm feeling well relaxed, and my mind is in its correct state after those drinks."

We finish our conversation, and I think we are slightly tipsy from the three glasses of wine we both had. Californian wine is smooth and sweet, but it will sneak up on you if you are not paying attention. We walk towards the elevator to our room, and I see this familiar guy walk past me. He gives me a smile as if he knows who I am as well. Wow, I wish I could remember who he is, but nothing is coming to mind. As we walk into the elevator, he turns around and catches the door with his hand.

"I'm sorry to intrude, but I couldn't help to think that I know you from some place. What is your name, if you don't mind me asking?"

"Jahanna."

"Jahanna, ahh yes hello. I am Christopher.

I turn towards Nia and squeeze her hand, whispering hard that this is the guy that I was telling her about. This is the Christopher. The elevator stops on the second floor, and Nia gets out. I was so blind by this mishaps that I forgot I stayed on this floor as well.

CAN YOU KEEP A SECRET?

"Jah, are you coming?"

"I don't think so", I replied.

CAN YOU KEEP A SECRET?

As women, we put ourselves last. If never a man was to know my value, then I sure want to. It's just hard picking up the pieces with a broken finger.